The Education System in England and Wales

John Dunford and Paul Sharp

LONGMAN
London and New York

Longman Group UK Limited,
Longman House, Burnt Mill, Harlow,
Essex CM20 2JE, England
and Associated Companies throughout the world.

First published 1990

British Library Cataloguing in Publication Data
Dunford, John
    The education system in England and Wales. –
(Effective teacher series) – (The effective teacher series)
    1. England. Education
    I. Title II. Sharp, Paul
    30.942

ISBN 0-582-00966-9

Library of Congress Cataloging-in-Publication Data
Dunford, J. R.
    The education system in England and Wales/by John
Dunford and Paul Sharp.
        p.   cm. – The Effective teacher series)
    Includes index.
    ISBN 0-582-00966-9 : £5.95
    1. Education – England – History. 2. Education –
Wales – History.
    I. Sharp, P. R. (Paul R.) II. Title. III. Series.
    LA631. D84 1990
    370'.944 – dc20   89-31394
                                                                    CIP

Set in 10/11pt Times Roman

Produced by Longman Group (FE) Limited
Printed in Hong Kong

THE EFFECTIVE TEACHER SERIES

General Editor: Elizabeth Perrott

CONTENTS

EDITOR'S PREFACE

This new series was inspired by my book on the practice of teaching (*Effective Teaching: a practical guide to improving your teaching*, Longman, 1982) written for teacher training students as well as for in-service teachers wishing to improve their teaching skills. The books in this series have been written with the same readership in mind. However, busy classroom teachers will also find that the books serve their needs as changes in the nature and pattern of education make the re-training of experienced teachers more essential than in the past.

The rationale behind the series is that professional courses for teachers require the coverage of a wide variety of subjects in a relatively short time. So the aim of the series is the production of 'easy to read', practical guides to provide the necessary subject background, supported by references to encourage and guide further reading together with questions and/or exercises devised to assist application and evaluation.

As specialists in their selected fields, the authors have been chosen for their ability to relate their subjects closely to the needs of teachers and to stimulate discussion of contemporary issues in education.

The series covers subjects ranging from *The Theory of Education* to *The Teaching of Mathematics* and from *The Psychology of Learning* to *Health Education*. It will look at aspects of education as diverse as *Education and Cultural Diversity* and *Assessment in Education; The Teaching of English* and *The History of Education*. Although some titles such as *The Administration of Education* are specific to England and Wales, the majority of titles, such as *Comparative Education, The Teaching of Modern Languages, The Use of Computers in Teaching* and *Pupil Welfare and Counselling* will be international in scope.

In a period when education is a subject of general debate and is operating against a background of major change, there is little doubt that the books, although of primary interest to teachers, will also find a wider readership.

Elizabeth Perrott

ACKNOWLEDGEMENTS

We are grateful to the following for permission to reproduce copyright material: The Controller of Her Majesty's Stationery Office for tables 5.1 & 5.2 from *The Statistical Bulletin 14/87* (Dec. 1987), tables 5.3 & 5.4 from *Teachers Pay and Conditions* (1988) and table 6.1 from *The Statistical Bulletin 14/88* (Dec. 1988).

LIST OF ABBREVIATIONS

AEC	Association of Education Committees
AFE	Advanced Further Education
BEC	Business Education Council
BTEC	Business and Technician Education Council
CATE	Council for the Accreditation of Teacher Education
CCTA	City College for the Technology of the Arts.
CEE	Certificate of Extended Education
CGLI	City and Guilds of London Institute
CNAA	Council for National Academic Awards
CPVE	Certificate of Pre-Vocational Education
CSE	Certificate of Secondary Education
CTC	City Technology College
DES	Department of Education and Science
FE	Further Education
GCE	General Certificate of Education
GCSE	General Certificate of Secondary Education
GRE	Grant Related Expenditure
HMI	Her Majesty's Inspectorate
ILEA	Inner London Education Authority
LEA	Local Education Authority
MSC	Manpower Services Commission
NAFE	Non-Advanced Further Education
NCC	National Curriculum Council
NCQV	National Council for Vocational Qualifications
NUT	National Union of Teachers
OECD	Organisation for Economic Cooperation and Development
PCFC	Polytechnics and Colleges Funding Council
RSA	Royal Society of Arts
RSG	Rate Support Grant
TEC	Technician Education Council
TEC	Training and Enterprise Council
TUC	Trades Union Congress

TVEI	Technical and Vocational Education Initiative
UFC	Universities Funding Council
UGC	University Grants Committee
WRNAFE	Work-Related Non-Advanced Further Education
YTS	Youth Training Scheme

LIST OF FIGURES

LIST OF TABLES

The development of the education service in the nineteenth and twentieth centuries

It is important to begin this book with a historical chapter because the roots of the present education system are so firmly embedded in the past. Although our system has some features of recent origin, certain of its most basic facets have survived directly and visibly from the nineteenth century. As you use this book, you will, from time to time, almost certainly find it helpful to refer back to this chapter either to remind yourself of the origins of a particular development or to try to work out why certain trends and traditions in the system have been so persistent and remained so dominant. In certain instances you may conclude that approaches and traditions, once firmly established, have lasted long after concerted attempts have been made to break them. In the nineteenth century, for example, the notion of elementary schools catering for the educational needs of the children of the poorer classes became so firmly established that the abolition of elementary schools as such in 1944 was unable to remove from our system this concept of education with its connotations of a particular kind of schooling for a specified social group. Some contemporary educationists would maintain that even in the post-war years some of our schools, despite their more modern names, were still constrained by elements of the persistent elementary tradition.

In the early nineteenth century this country was not a democracy, and to understand the early measures to promote the education of the poorer classes it is necessary to consider the attitudes of the influential social groups (some would use the term 'the propertied governing classes') because they were in the positions of power and controlled the available resources. Some members of these influential groups took up a reactionary stance. They believed that educating the poor would easily stir them up and make them discontented with their lot in life. There were still vivid memories of the disruption of the French Revolution, and the processes of industrialisation and urbanisation in this country implied rapid change and seemed to threaten stability. This group believed that the role of the State should be confined to foreign policy, the preservation of law and order and the administration of justice. They did not even contemplate that in the future the

State might become involved in active economic and social policies. On the question of educating the children of the poor, they believed in 'letting sleeping dogs lie'. Other members of the influential social classes adopted rather different attitudes to this issue. Like the first group, they wanted to preserve the status quo, but they believed in different means to achieve this end. They took the view that if the children of the poor were provided with an education which stressed certain qualities such as obedience to authority and virtues such as hard work they would begin to respect the order of the world in which they lived. Religious instruction was seen as of paramount importance, probably partly because in many respects this provided a particular kind of social education as well as Bible stories. The motives were predominantly paternalistic, and there is little doubt that in this period the provision of education for the children of the poor was seen as an important means of social control. This does not deny, however, that some paternalists were much more 'benevolent' than others. Some of them were certainly motivated by genuinely religious, philanthropic and humanitarian feelings. They believed that education could promote greater social cohesion and could lead to real understanding and harmony between different social classes. Such people accepted that some reforms were necessary and that there was plenty of scope for improvement in the conditions of life of the ordinary folk. They did not rule out changes, but they believed that these had to take place within the context of an ordered, stable and stratified social system. They hoped that providing education for some of the working class might help to reduce social, economic and political conflicts which seemed to threaten Britain's emerging industrial and urban society.

During the early years of the nineteenth century the Churches were responsible for organising much of the education provided for children of the poor although the contribution of working-class private schools, including dame schools, has often been underestimated and maligned. Although the strictly educational achievements of the dame schools were probably limited, there is evidence that they provided a much needed and appreciated child-minding service within their local communities. Many of the Church schools were operated on the lines of the monitorial system which involved some of the older and more able children teaching the younger pupils. It enabled one schoolmaster to keep a comparatively large school under his scrutiny. Instruction was normally restricted to the three Rs with perhaps some needle-work for girls. Emphasis was placed upon discipline and good order and religion was provided by reading from the Bible and other means. In this period the Churches were keen to extend their educational work and they set up new organisations to promote these developments. In 1811 the Anglicans formed the National Society for Promoting the Education of the Poor in the Principles of the Established Church, and three years later the non-conformists followed with their British and Foreign School Society. The National Society's efforts produced more schools and reached more children. The denominational rivalry, implicit in the existence of these two competing societies, soon became firmly embedded in the education system, and it was not until well into the twentieth century that the schools finally escaped from its influence. The Churches, therefore, were providing assistance to schools in this country before the State became involved. Before the Government had paid out a penny, these voluntary bodies had raised their own funds, built their own schools and employed their own teachers. In these circumstances it is perhaps not surprising that the Churches have sought to retain an important place in the education service ever since.

A number of parliamentary bills aimed at aiding the education of the lower orders from public funds was introduced in the first three decades of the nineteenth century. Contemporaries in Parliament often regarded these proposed measures as over-ambitious in educational terms, but also found the problems concerning the provision of religious education intractable. It was not until 1833 that an important breakthrough occurred. In that year Parliament voted a grant of £20,000 to assist the building of elementary schools. For the first time public money was channelled into schooling. To qualify for a grant promoters of schools had to show that they had raised at least half of the total cost from voluntary contributions and the application had to be supported by either the National Society or the British and Foreign School Society. At this stage no grants were paid towards the running costs of schools. The Treasury was responsible for distributing these building grants as no education department had yet been created. This very limited system of aid existed for a period of six years, and the evidence suggests that the lion's share of these grants went on subsidising the building of Church of England schools.

By the end of the 1830s there were pressures to increase and to broaden the scope of the grants to elementary education and, at the same time, there was a need to put the existing system of aid on to a firmer and more regular footing. The obvious solution was to create a department of state for education, but the government of the day feared that the introduction of such a proposal into Parliament would stir up old religious rivalries and jealousies. To avoid this problem, it proceeded in an unusual way. By Order in Council it set up a Committee of the Privy Council for Education (hereafter called 'the Committee') without recourse to legislation. The Committee consisted of four members: the Lord President of the Council, the Lord Privy Seal, the Chancellor of the Exchequer and the Home Secretary.[1] Between the meetings of the Committee, the Lord President took responsibility for educational business. He was assisted in this by the Committee's newly appointed Secretary, who was a senior civil servant. The first person to hold this office was James Kay-Shuttleworth who soon proved to be an active and influential educational innovator. The strange way in which the Committee emerged and its unusual constitutional position soon led to difficulties, for its existence tended to blur rather than clarify those who had ultimate responsibility for the development of aid to education. During the 1840s and 1850s the range of grants available for elementary schools was considerably extended, and, by the mid-1850s, members of the Commons were increasingly concerned about their lack of direct contact with the Committee particularly as its expenditure was growing rapidly. The Committee did not have to seek parliamentary authority to introduce new grants, and the Commons had little chance to review or criticise its work. Despite the continued fears of senior civil servants that the involvement of Parliament in the closer scrutiny of the Committee's system of aid would lead to even more denominational wrangling, members were, by this time, convinced of the need for a legislative framework for the machinery to control education. In 1856 an Act was passed which created the post of Vice-President of the Committee. The holder of this office became a member of the Committee and was made the minister responsible to the Commons for all matters connected with education. This change made the executive responsible to Parliament for its educational policies and grants and a much more clearly defined Education Department was set up in Whitehall. These constitutional arrangements lasted, with only minor amendments, until the end of the nineteenth century.

As early as 1839 the Committee made two important changes in the scope of State aid. Firstly, it indicated that it would make grants to schools that were outside the control of the two great societies, and by 1847 some of the schools under the purview of the Roman Catholic Poor School Committee were receiving financial assistance from the State. Secondly, the Committee began to offer aid towards the recurrent expenditure of schools. Before this only building grants had been available, and this change marked a most important innovation. Over the next twenty years the Committee distributed a range of different 'fertilising' grants for the benefit of the schools and total central government assistance to elementary education increased dramatically from about £30,000 in 1839 to over £800,000 in 1859.[2] The Committee made it clear in 1839 that it could not give grants to schools without ensuring that the conditions of aid were met and that the schools operated efficiently. There had to be some checks that regulations were obeyed and that value for money was obtained. The Committee proposed to appoint inspectors to deal with these matters. Initially, the Church of England opposed the introduction of government inspectors and a dispute between the established Church and the State ensued. In 1840 a concordat was negotiated and it was conceded that the Church would have influence over those who were appointed to inspect its schools. Consequently for a period of thirty years the inspectorate operated on a denominational basis. The duties of inspectors were both administrative and educational, and, from the outset, there were differences of view about how far the role of inspectors should be advisory and how far inquisitorial. Most of the early inspectors were graduates of the ancient universities and some of them were clergymen. Very few had experience of teaching in elementary schools. Over the years the inspectorate has expanded and the roles it performs in the education service have become more complex. To this day Her Majesty's Inspectorate (HMI) of Schools remains an important and influential component in the control and development of the educational system.

The most significant innovation introduced by the Committee's first Secretary, James Kay-Shuttleworth, was the pupil-teacher system. This was introduced in 1846 and attempted, with some success, to solve the crucial problems of teacher training and supply in elementary education. Suitable young people, who had normally been educated in elementary schools, were selected at about the age of thirteen (social, moral and intellectual criteria were all employed in the selection process) to become apprentices or pupil-teachers. These young people received some financial assistance from Government to work for five years in elementary schools as young trainee teachers. The head teachers of the schools provided instruction for their pupil-teachers after school hours and received payment for this. If, at the end of their apprenticeship, pupil-teachers passed their examinations in academic subjects and practical teaching, they became qualified teachers in their own right. Some of the more able pupil-teachers competed for Queen's scholarships which took the successful candidates to residential colleges provided by the denominational bodies for two years for further education and training. The pupil-teacher system offered able young people from ordinary working-class homes the opportunity to enter stable and respectable employment. Although the status of elementary school teaching was never particularly high, some young people probably saw a career in teaching as a means of 'getting on' and perhaps regarded it as upward social mobility of a minor kind. The evidence suggests that few from the poorer sections of the working class became pupil-teachers, but this system became an important avenue to professional employment for young people, especially girls, from solid working-class backgrounds. The pupil-teacher system remained crucial to the supply and training of elementary school teachers throughout the nineteenth century, and, indeed, it continued to exist into the early years of this century.

Nineteenth-century elementary education in this country is normally and correctly associated in the public mind with payment on results. This system was introduced by the then Vice-President of the Committee, Robert Lowe, in the Revised Code of 1862. The term 'Code' requires a short explanation. From 1860 until the end of the century the Education Department issued its 'Code' annually, and this set out in some detail the rules, regulations and grants currently in force. Historians of education find the Revised Code a lively issue and its causes and effects are still discussed and debated with considerable vigour on all sides. It will not be possible in this book to address the many complex issues that have been raised in these debates, and only a brief outline can be provided. In 1862 the government of the day wanted to simplify its aid to elementary schools. Partly because administration had become so cumbersome, it withdrew several of its 'fertilising' grants. At about the same time it curtailed some of its assistance to pupil-teachers. Some historians have seen these measures as a concerted attempt by Robert Lowe to reduce public expenditure on elementary education, but others question whether he had such intentions. To replace the old grants, elementary schools could earn twelve shillings (60p) for every child over six years of age who made a required number of attendances as verified by the inspectors. Each child, however, was to be examined in the three Rs, and two shillings and eight pence per subject per child was deducted from payments if the examinations were failed. The children were graded into six standards for these examinations and no pupil could be entered at more than one level or repeat a standard already successfully passed. The inspectors (or more accurately their assistants) normally conducted these examinations as the main part of their annual visits. There can be little doubt that this system put considerable pressure on teachers and children. For a time it tended to narrow the school curriculum to the three Rs, but as the Code was amended, other subjects were added. To some extent, these new arrangements made this aspect less important after the 1860s. From the outset, the system of payment on results was controversial, but it was to dominate central government aid to elementary education until the early 1890s and has been held responsible for introducing and perpetuating a restrictive pedagogy emphasising drill and rote learning. It has been suggested that payment on results made teachers cram their pupils in a mindless fashion for the annual examinations so that grants could be maximised. Although some writers now take a much less negative view of payment on results, there can be little doubt that this system became a deeply engrained feature of the elementary school tradition. Some educationists have argued that it was well into the twentieth century before this country's educational system really escaped from the restricting and debilitating effects of payment on results. Others maintain that, for its time, payment on results was an ingenious and effective mechanism for providing aid to elementary schools, and that its longer term negative effects have been much exaggerated. It is probably significant that payment on results was widely employed in providing State aid to the elementary and technical education intended for the working classes. In contrast, the private sectors of education serving higher social groups made little use of payment on results. Different systems of finance, which certainly were not without their educational consequences, served, therefore, to reinforce the existing divides.

There is some evidence from the 1860s that educational provisions were expanding relatively rapidly and that illiteracy was diminishing. Between 1863 and 1869 over 1,000 new elementary schools were opened, and more children were in attendance for longer periods and with more regularity than formerly. One commentator has argued that the existing voluntary system was making such considerable progress that, given time and increased central government aid, further radical changes were unnecessary.[3] With minor modifications, the voluntary system could cope with the educational requirements of an advanced industrial country. This, however, is only part of the story. There was increasing evidence from the large towns and cities that large numbers of children in some districts were receiving little, if any, education at all. In some cities children who were neither in school nor in jobs were becoming a nuisance on the streets. They often became involved in petty crime and posed a threat to law and order. In the schools far more children were in lower standards than higher, which strongly suggests a short period of education for the majority. The Churches, for obvious reasons, had greater difficulty in raising funds for schools in the poorer parts of industrial cities than in the countryside and in market towns, and the industrial areas were those in greatest need of schools. During the later 1860s there were increasing pressures for a major measure to extend educational provisions. The child population was still increasing rapidly, and there were concerns about social order if children were not occupied either in school or in employment. For many years some non-conformists who were popularly known as 'Voluntarists' (largely Congregationalists with some Baptists) were totally opposed to all forms of State assistance to education. They held that State involvement in education was a potential threat to political and religious liberties, and they attempted to run schools in connection with their chapels on a self-financing basis. By the late 1860s they were forced to admit that their endeavours had failed, and they now wanted the State to promote education in ways other than through subsidies to the voluntary schools. In the same period economic and political factors began to make educational reform more likely. The Paris Exhibition of 1867 illustrated that Britain now had important industrial rivals and the emerging Germany seemed a particular threat to Britain's economic supremacy. The Reform Act of the same year extended the franchise to male householders in the towns, and some felt that it was now essential to ensure that, as far as possible, potential new voters were supplied with some basic education. In the late 1860s a number of education bills were introduced into Parliament but they all failed. It was the election of a Liberal Government with a working majority at the end of 1868 that made major educational legislation a realistic possibility.

In 1870 W. E. Forster, the radical Vice-President of the Committee, and his Liberal colleagues produced this country's first major education act. Forster told the Commons that the Government's main objective was to 'complete the present voluntary system, to fill up the gaps'.[4] A grasp of this limited aim is crucial to an understanding of the English educational system in the last quarter of the nineteenth century. There was certainly no intention to destroy or damage the existing voluntary schools, and indeed, an important concomitant of the 1870 Act was a significant increase in central government aid to all elementary schools. Each borough – and, in the countryside, each parish – was required to conduct an inquiry into the facilities available for elementary education in its area. Returns were then made to the Education Department. If there was a deficiency of school places, the voluntary societies were given a period of six months to make up the shortage. During this time building grants from central government remained available, but it was made clear that they would be withdrawn at the end of 1870. This induced a considerable burst of building activity. If the voluntary bodies failed to make up the deficiency in an area, arrangements for the election of a school board had to be made. Many of the larger boroughs moved quickly to set up School Boards, although in more rural areas the pace was often much slower because of the fears of the expense involved. School Boards were given extensive powers to provide, equip, maintain and staff elementary schools. They were empowered to raise rates to finance these activities.

Although School Boards did not come into existence everywhere (in a few boroughs and a large number of parishes there were sufficient school places in the voluntary sector), they were this country's first Local Education Authorities (LEAs). All ratepayers (male and female) had the vote in School Board elections and men and women were equally eligible for election. School Boards provided women with their first opportunities to take part in the democratic process in this country. Unlike present LEAs, School Boards were 'ad hoc' authorities. They were elected solely to deal with educational issues, and some would claim that this was one of their most important characteristics. Some educationists believe that it was an advantage that School Board members could channel all their energies into education and that they were not distracted by non-educational factors as can happen when education is administered by a committee of a multi-purpose local authority. It is sometimes suggested that 'ad hoc' authorities would administer our present education service rather better than our existing local structures.

The School Boards, particularly in the urban areas, set to work with considerable purpose. New schools were built and staff engaged. By 1880 attendance at school was made compulsory for all children. The School Boards, with access to rates, were soon outstripping the voluntary schools, which still relied on subscriptions, in terms of annual expenditure per child. Often the larger Boards offered higher salaries to teachers, and they tended to attract the best-qualified staff. Once 'the gaps were filled', some of the urban Boards began to extend their activities beyond a limited conception of elementary education. Large higher grade schools, which were neo-secondary in nature, were established in a number of cities and towns, and by the 1890s these Boards were justly proud of their achievements in this area. Taking into account the problems they had to overcome, the educational progress made by some School Boards in a relatively short period of about twenty-five years is remarkable.

From the mid-nineteenth century the State began to take an interest in post-elementary education. As the primary purpose of this was to promote Britain's industrial performance in an endeavour to keep this country competitive in world markets, aid to technical education for artisans preceded grants for secondary schools. In the 1830s and 1840s a number of schools of design were set up, and Government gave subsidies to these institutions to provide part-time instruction to artisans in technical art- and design-related subjects. Following the Great Exhibition of 1851 a new government organisation, the Science and Art Department, was formed in 1853. It took over and amended the existing scheme of aid to these art schools, and introduced grants for the scientific instruction of working people. In its early years the Science and Art Department worked under the auspices of the Board of Trade, but in 1856 it was transferred to the Committee.

Throughout its existence it operated from South Kensington and remained completely separate from the Education Department in Whitehall. By the 1860s the Science and Art Department had instituted a relatively successful system of payment on examination results in a range of scientific and artistic subjects normally taken by working people on a part-time basis in the evening. This teaching was usually undertaken by part-timers who held other posts in the day, and the classes were held in a wide variety of buildings including the premises of elementary schools, mechanics' institutes and similar voluntary associations. The Department always insisted that it taught the scientific principles which underlay industrial activities, and it conformed to the prevailing Victorian *laissez-faire* ideology that State involvement in economic matters should be avoided as much as possible. During the 1860s and early 1870s the Department's work grew very rapidly, and, although progress was less spectacular after this, there was a further upsurge in activity during the 1890s. By the last quarter of the nineteenth century some politicians and a few industrialists were concerned that this country's provisions for technical education were less adequate than those of its industrial rivals. Pressure was put on Parliament to do something about this issue. At first there were problems because some Conservatives would not countenance giving powers in post-elementary education to the School Boards that were increasingly seen as a Liberal 'sphere of influence' in the cities. In 1888, however, multi-purpose local authorities, the county councils and county borough councils, were set up, and the following year these new authorities were granted permissive powers to raise a penny rate for technical education. There was no rush on the part of most authorities to implement this measure, but in 1890 a windfall to technical education transformed the situation. To extricate itself from certain political difficulties, the government of the day made substantial sums, commonly known as 'whisky money grants' available to the local authorities for technical education. These proved, for their time, to be comparatively generous annual payments, and most authorities quickly set up technical instruction committees to organise schemes of aid. The term 'technical instruction' was interpreted widely, and in the 1890s a number of progressive local authorities, using these new central government grants, began to develop extensive ranges of provisions in the post-elementary field.

The State's involvement in secondary education was much more limited. Secondary schools remained fee-paying institutions catering almost exclusively for the children of the upper and middle classes. The State, through the Charity Commission, ensured that endowments were properly administered, but no central government grants were made to secondary schools as such. From the 1880s some grammar schools entered some of their pupils for Science and Art Department examinations and earned income in this way. At the local level some of the more ambitious urban School Boards developed higher grade schools which, in practice, provided secondary schooling for older scholars. The higher grade schools also made extensive use of the Science and Art Department's scheme of aid, and some large and highly successful schools emerged in the 1890s on this basis. During the last decade of the century, the technical instruction committees began to aid secondary schools for their work in scientific, technical and commercial subjects. Although the more richly endowed schools could afford to ignore these developments, many grammar schools were prepared to adapt their curricula to qualify for the grants now offered. Even at the end of the century, however, assistance from public funds to secondary schools came on a piecemeal basis, and it was widely recognised that more organisation and coordination were required in this sector of education. In Wales the situation was more satisfactory than in England because of the Welsh Intermediate Act of 1889. This measure had created joint education committees for secondary education, and money raised from rates was supplemented by central government grants. The principality, which had comparatively few endowed schools, was thus enabled to develop its secondary schooling.

The years at the end of the nineteenth century and the beginning of the twentieth, are crucial for understanding education in this country for it was during this period that our present system was forged. By the 1890s there was a number of pressing issues awaiting urgent solutions.

At central government level there were three departments administering education. Both the Education Department and the Science and Art Department had major responsibilities, with the Charity Commission involved to a lesser extent. In the localities there was a wide range of education authorities. Over 2,500 School Boards, which it must be stressed did not exist everywhere, provided elementary education (and in certain cases encouraged post-elementary developments), and over 100 technical instruction committees, which were almost universal and formed part of multi-purpose local authorities, were often developing their educational work quickly and successfully. In addition, there were hundreds of governing bodies of secondary schools and no fewer than 14,000 separate managing bodies for voluntary elementary schools. Administrative reform was urgent as there was little coordination between the different bodies providing education at this time.

Educational issues also required attention. There was consensus that local authorities should take charge of secondary education, but there were deep differences of opinion about whether powers in this area should be given to the School Boards or to the multi-purpose local authorities. The financial plight of the voluntary schools became increasingly serious throughout the 1890s. Voluntary schools were already well behind the leading School Boards in terms of annual expenditure per child, and in a number of instances managers gave up the struggle for funds and allowed boards to take over their schools. In material terms many voluntary schools were providing a second-class elementary education. Despite attempts to bolster up the poorest voluntary schools with extra financial assistance from the State, it was clear towards the end of the 1890s that only major reform could ensure the survival of the voluntary schools in the long term.

Political factors were of considerable importance in the recasting of the education system. By the 1890s the School Boards, because of their composition in the urban areas, were widely linked in the public mind with the Liberal Party and non-conformity. The Liberals certainly tended to look after their interests in Parliament. In contrast, and perhaps inevitably, the Conservatives normally took up the cause of the voluntary schools. They regarded many of the School Boards as over-ambitious and extravagant, and argued that the Boards' access to rates put the voluntary schools at perpetual financial disadvantage. They stressed that the supporters of voluntary schools had to come up with their contributions to their own schools and then pay rates to support their rivals. The Conservatives won power nationally in 1895 and retained it until 1906. This had a considerable bearing on the reforms made in education. The Government and its senior civil servants, who soon included Robert Morant above all responsible for the detailed work on the major changes, were determined that the technical instruction committees should be established as the dominant authorities in post-elementary education and that the School Boards should be severely confined to the elementary sector. Eventually, those working against the School Boards questioned the London School Board's rights to provide post-elementary education in the courts and the famous Cockerton Judgement went in their favour. The Government rushed through a bill so that in the short term the Boards' post-elementary work could continue as long as permission for it was received from the appropriate county or borough council. For the longer term the Government embarked on major administrative and educational reforms.

In 1899 the Board of Education Act was passed. The powers of the Education Department, the Science and Art Department and the Charity Commission (as far as they related to education) were transferred to the new Board, which became a consolidated central department of education. The President of the Board was, in effect, the Minister of Education. For a few years the old divisions between Whitehall and South Kensington persisted as strongly as before, but soon after Morant was appointed Permanent Secretary in 1903 much more coordination and consolidation were achieved. In many ways this measure has been overshadowed by the fundamental changes made by the Education Act of 1902.

The Bill of 1902 aroused much more immediate public opposition than any other educational measure in this country's history. Controversy focused on one main issue – the proposal to aid Church elementary schools from the rates. The Liberals and the non-conformists were outraged and massive demonstrations against 'Rome on the rates' took place. Wales, led by Lloyd George, was particularly incensed, and even after the Act was passed opposition continued. For a time some Welsh authorities refused to pay grants to Church schools, and in parts of England such as West Yorkshire, where non-conformity was also strong, reaction was only marginally less extreme. In both Wales and England individual ratepayers refused to pay the education rate and were fined and had property distrained. After several years feelings cooled, and, although the Liberal Government of 1906 initially tried to undo the Act, it eventually became reconciled to retaining the measure.

This spectacular but relatively short-lived controversy should not blind us to the long-term importance of Morant's Act of 1902. The School Boards were abolished and their powers and assets transferred to new LEAs which covered the whole country. The county and county borough councils became new authorities for both elementary and post-elementary education, and Morant wanted these to be the only authorities. Political pressure, however, forced him to make a concession, and, under Part III of the Act, the councils of non-county boroughs with populations over 10,000 and urban districts over 20,000 were given responsibilities for elementary education only. Morant always had misgivings about this division of educational jurisdiction in certain towns, and there can be little doubt that problems in educational administration arose because of the operation of two separate authorities responsible for different sectors of education in some places. From 1902 there were over 300 local education authorities in existence, and about 200 of these worked under Part III in elementary education only. The new system of LEAs introduced by the Act was more simplified and streamlined than that which had caused complications and confusion in the 1890s. The new authorities were required to set up education committees in accordance with schemes approved by the Board of Education. These committees consisted of members of council and persons co-opted to serve because of their experience of education. It was required that women as well as men were on the committees. The numerical strengths of the various groups were not laid down, and different authorities developed rather different practices and traditions in this respect. In the first instance county authorities often built on their experience gained with technical instruction committees. There was normally some continuity in the membership of the committees and key officers usually remained in their posts with amended job descriptions.

The multi-purpose local authorities now owned, maintained, financed and operated a large number of 'provided' schools. The voluntary schools, which remained the property and responsibility of their managers, were now known as 'non-provided schools'. All the costs of non-provided schools, except capital developments, were borne by the local education authorities that controlled their secular instruction. From 1902 one-third of voluntary school managers were appointed by the LEA, but denominational interests retained their majority. Religious instruction remained under the control of the managers, as did the appointment of teachers. In return, for much greater financial assistance, the voluntary schools were incorporated further into the State education system. They continued to retain rights and freedoms which their supporters regarded as essential to their future existence, development and identity.

The changes in administrative structures and in elementary education have overshadowed the important measures for post-elementary education contained in the 1902 Act. The new authorities (excluding the Part IIIs as already explained) were given permissive powers to spend up to the limit of a two penny rate on 'education other than elementary'. In effect, this made them the local authorities for secondary education, and, in addition to making grants to existing schools, many LEAs started almost immediately to build and provide their own secondary schools. A few of the more progressive LEAs also used their powers to set up teacher training colleges which provided an important supplement to the voluntary colleges already in existence. The work of the technical instruction committees was consolidated in the years after 1902, and in a number of areas LEAs gave sizeable grants to neighbouring universities. Thus, within a short period, several of the larger and more dynamic LEAs were providing a wide range of educational services to their communities.

Some LEAs made particularly determined efforts to improve facilities for secondary education in their areas after 1902. Secondary schools remained fee-paying institutions, and they continued to provide their pupils with a predominantly academic education. In 1907 the Liberal Government introduced the free-place regulations which required all secondary schools in receipt of Board of Education grants to offer 25 per cent of their available places to able pupils from elementary schools. Some LEAs extended their scholarship provisions well beyond this minimum. The proportion of ex-elementary school pupils on scholarships in secondary schools increased sharply in the years before the First World War and again in the 1920s. In the early 1930s, however, because of policies of economic retrenchment, little advance was made. Scholarships were normally awarded on the basis of performance in examinations taken at eleven which, in practice, were highly competitive. Until the end of the First World War secondary schools were eligible for aid from both the Board of Education and their LEA, but from 1919 they were required to opt for one form of assistance or the other. Schools which chose central government aid were removed from LEA influence and became 'direct grant' schools. A number of famous grammar schools with high prestige opted for this status. Although grammar schools had existed for centuries, many of the new institutions set up by LEAs after 1902 were designated simply as 'secondary schools'. It was not until the late 1920s and 1930s that these schools – encouraged by the Hadow Report to differentiate themselves more clearly from the senior schools emerging under the elementary regulations – changed their titles and incorporated the term 'grammar' in their names. The statistics show that the number of pupils in secondary schools increased three-fold between 1902 and 1939. Some of this increase must be attributed to the expansion of scholarships, but the numbers of fee-payers also grew. Increases in real income during the First World War provided more parents with the means to buy secondary schooling for their offspring. Employment opportunities in white-collar jobs were still expanding and provided an outlet for pupils. It must be remembered that even in the depressed inter-war years those who remained in regular work enjoyed improvements in real income as prices fell further than wages and salaries. These economic changes enabled larger numbers of the lower middle classes to purchase places in secondary schools for their children.

Despite the expansion in secondary schools, before 1945 the elementary schools continued to provide the only form of education received by the vast majority of people in this country. Even in the years before 1914 the Board of Education and a number of LEAs in England and Wales were concerned about the older and more able pupils in elementary schools who merely repeated earlier work and who seemed generally 'to mark time' during their last years of schooling. In several authorities the elementary school curriculum was reviewed and extended, and, in particular, facilities for practical subjects such as cookery and woodwork were developed. London and Manchester took the lead in initiating more ambitious projects. Central schools were set up for able pupils not moving on to secondary schools. Although these operated under the elementary regulations, they were neo-secondary in nature normally catering for pupils aged eleven to fifteen, and they often included an industrial or commercial bias in their curricula. They had a number of features in common with the higher grade schools of the 1890s, and they were at the height of their popularity in the 1920s. They were much less common in areas such as the West Riding of Yorkshire where the authority concentrated on building up the scholarships to its secondary schools. The Board of Education's technical regulations were used in a rather similar fashion to build up post-elementary provisions for junior technical or trade schools, which normally recruited at thirteen. These were set up in several districts to prepare pupils for employment in local trades or industries.

The Education Act of 1918 raised the school-leaving age to 14, and further required LEAs to make provisions for senior elementary pupils (those aged 11 or over) in separate schools or classes. Progress with this issue proved difficult for many LEAs because of the cuts in public expenditure which followed the slump of 1921. Meanwhile, the Left, led by R. H. Tawney, was developing new concepts. In *Secondary Education for All*[5] Tawney argued that the largely separate subsystems of education in this country (secondary for the middle class, elementary for the working class) were archaic, divisive, socially unjust and no longer met the needs of the nation. He was certainly not satisfied with the provisions for neo-secondary education for working-class children that were being developed under the elementary and technical regulations. Tawney advocated that all children should attend primary schools until the age of 11 when they should all transfer to secondary schools where their education would continue to be provided free of charge. Many of these issues were considered further in the Hadow Report, *The Education of the Adolescent*, published at the end of 1926[6]. It stressed that many educational opportunities were still missed during the last years of compulsory elementary schooling and proposed that there should be a break at 11 in the education of all children. It further suggested that the school-leaving age should be raised to 15, although, with hindsight, we know that this was not achieved until after the Second World War. Children over the age of 11, who did not go on to secondary grammar schools, were to receive their post-primary education in 'modern' or 'secondary modern' schools which were to be developed from existing central schools, senior schools and senior classes (sometimes called senior or higher 'tops'). These modern schools were to be encouraged to develop their own distinctive curricula which were to be considerably less academic than the provisions in the grammar schools. The Report's intention for the long term was that modern schools would be completely separate institutions from schools educating children under eleven, but, in the short term, it was acknowledged that in most cases existing elementary schools would have to be reorganised into two departments, the first serving the needs of the younger children and the second the older. The Board of Education accepted the recommendations of the Hadow Report and urged LEAs to reorganise on the lines suggested. Some additional funding was provided, and throughout the 1930s LEAs put considerable effort into reorganisation. Progress varied from area to area according to the intensity of the problems encountered. In districts where there were significant numbers of voluntary schools the Churches were unwilling to lose pupils at the age of 11, but found raising funds for the necessary capital developments very difficult. Although the Education Act of 1936 offered grant aid towards the building of denominational modern schools, this change came too late to make much impact before the outbreak of war. In towns where different Part II and Part III authorities were existing side by side but controlling separate sectors of education, there were sometimes political and administrative barriers which caused delays in reorganisation. In general, rural areas posed more problems than urban ones because of their widely dispersed child populations. Additionally, the economic climate of the 1930s, particularly as it affected public expenditure, was hardly conducive to educational change and development. Nonetheless, by 1938 over 50 per cent of all elementary pupils over 11 were being educated in reorganised senior schools or departments. All-age elementary schools were, at last, losing their dominance in English and Welsh education. In many respects these changes made in the 1930s pointed the way to how schooling would be organised in the years after the war.

The Second World War caused some dislocation in the educational service. Evacuation, staff shortages and suspension of building programmes all created their own problems. War also brought important changes in social attitudes, and across a range of government activities and services there was determination to plan for a better future. Planning for educational reconstruction culminated in the Coalition Government's Education Act of 1944 and much of the credit for this measure is normally given to R. A. Butler, President of the Board of Education. The 1944 Act was by far the most important piece of educational legislation since 1902, and in many ways it still remains the basis of our current educational system. The broad outlines of this measure will be discussed in this chapter, but some of the more detailed ramifications of this Act will be considered, as appropriate, in later sections of the book.

The 1944 Act abolished the Board of Education replacing it as the central authority with a new Ministry of Education. The new Minister was put into a position where greater initiative could be and was at times taken from the centre. In a number of respects the independence of LEAs was under the ultimate control and direction of the Minister. LEAs, for example, were given several new statutory duties, but the Minister was charged with ensuring that they were carried out and he/she could impose and direct if LEAs failed to meet their obligations. As a result of the changes of 1944 there was more unity and standardisation in the national education service, and perhaps even a small reduction in the grosser disparities in educational opportunities between different parts of the country although this is questioned by a number of educationists. Nonetheless, local variations still remained a basic feature of this country's education system. Later, in 1964, the Ministry of Education was in its turn replaced by the Department of Education and Science (DES). As the name implies this brought education and science under the control of one administrative body. At the same time the DES took over from the Treasury certain responsibilities for the universities. The Secretary of State for Education and Science is the political head of the Department and is a cabinet minister who is assisted by a small number of junior ministers with responsibilities for particular sectors of the education service. Responsibilities for schools in Wales were transferred to the Welsh Office in 1970. Eight years later Welsh further education followed the schools.

Changes in local administration were also made in the 1944 Act. Part III authorities were abolished and county borough councils (about 150 in all) now remained the only LEAs. Although in a number of counties divisional executives were set up and exercised some relatively minor administrative functions, they were never rivals to the major authorities and were abolished in 1974. From 1944 all secondary schools were required to have governing bodies and all primary schools managing bodies. In some authorities schools were treated individually, but in others the practice of grouping a number of schools (in some cases a large number) of the same type under one governing or managing body continued. The powers, influences and energies of governing and managing bodies varied considerably from one authority to another.

The position of the voluntary schools was amended. Two major categories were devised – voluntary controlled and voluntary aided schools. In the case of the former all financial responsibilities were transferred to the LEA which appointed two-thirds of the governing (or managing) body. Voluntary aided schools remained much more denominational in character. The voluntary body still nominated two-thirds of the governing body and could continue to provide denominational instruction and worship. The governing body retained the responsibility for appointing teachers although appointments had to be ratified by the LEA. On the other hand, the voluntary body had to find 50 per cent (later reduced in stages to 15 per cent) of the capital costs of new buildings, alterations and external repairs. In general the Roman Catholics opted for aided status for their schools, but a greater proportion of Church of England schools became controlled. Since 1944 voluntary controlled and ordinary maintained county schools have been similar in almost all respects. Religious worship and instruction were compulsory in all schools, but in county and voluntary controlled schools these activities had to be undenominational. Parents who wished to withdraw their children from religious assemblies or lessons could do so. It was largely assumed in 1944 that the terms 'religious' and 'Christian' were synonymous, but social changes in post-war Britain have brought radical alterations to religious education in schools. Current practice has very little connection with the issues which dominated the policy-makers in the mid-1940s.

In 1944 the concept of elementary education was dropped, and LEAs were required to organise their provisions into three successive stages – primary, secondary and further. They were directed to prepare and submit development plans to the Ministry for approval. Although in the longer term these development plans were often largely discarded, in the late 1940s much effort was put into them. Primary and secondary education were to be provided in separate schools and children were to transfer from one stage to the other at the age of 11. Fees were abolished in all maintained secondary schools, and the school-leaving age was to be raised initially to 15 (achieved in 1947) and eventually to 16 (after considerable delay this was attained in 1972). The Act indicated that children should be educated according to their ages, abilities and aptitudes, but no attempt was made to define 'abilities and aptitudes'. Later attempts by post-war educators to interpret these terms in the context of secondary education and in the light of their own social and political values led to deep differences of opinion. In many ways the Act of 1944 provided no more than signposts for the post-war era, for in several crucial areas it was very much a product of the concerns and compromises of the 1940s. It remained, for example, silent on the future organisation of secondary schooling, but, implicitly, it seemed to look back to the dominant thinking of the late 1920s and 1930s. It removed the idea of elementary education without indicating how primary schools would be very different. In further education it did provide for the creation of county colleges which were to supply compulsory part-time education for the fifteen-to eighteen-years range, but, this radical proposal, admittedly first mooted in a slightly different form in 1918, was never implemented. The Act of 1944 consolidated and established several new principles, but it was unrealistic to expect it to transform the education system at a stroke. It is now necessary to consider how this major legislation affected the development of the service in the thirty years after the war.

Whatever the nation planned for the future, in the short term it was obliged to operate the education system which it inherited from the pre-war period. Shortages of materials and labour prevented rapid progress with building programmes being made. The sharp increase in the birth rate meant that there were far more children to be educated, and, to make matters more difficult, there was already a shortage of teachers. In the late 1940s priority had to be given to the emergency teacher training scheme and to the provision of 'roofs over heads'. Class sizes continued to remain large in both primary and secondary schools. As fast as possible LEAs began to try to phase out all-age ex-elementary schools and reorganise them into separate primary and secondary accommodation. This proved a difficult task, particularly in rural areas with large numbers of denominational schools, and it was not until the early 1960s that the vestiges of pre-war elementary school organisation were finally removed.

The organisation of secondary schooling soon proved the most controversial educational issue in the post-war period. During the 1930s the education system had utilised at least three types of secondary or neo-secondary schools. There were the grammar schools, the junior technical schools – which the Spens Report[7] of 1938 had suggested should be converted to technical high schools, recruiting at the age of eleven – and the senior or secondary modern schools which had emerged from the Hadow reorganisation. Although senior civil servants in the elementary branch of the Board of Education wanted to see more unity in secondary education after the war, those in the secondary branch favoured the retention of the different kinds of secondary provision.[8] Eventually the views of the secondary branch proved more influential. In 1943 a committee under the Chairmanship of Sir Cyril Norwood, an ex-public school headmaster, postulated that children could be divided broadly into three categories according to 'types of mind'. There were the academic children who were interested in 'learning for its own sake' and suitable for grammar schools; there were those with interests in 'applied science or applied art' who could attend secondary technical schools, and there were the others who dealt 'more easily with concrete things than ideas' and who could be accommodated best in the secondary modern schools. It was in the 1930s and in the Norwood Report[9] that the origins of the famous tripartite system were to be found. The Act of 1944 in no way committed the nation to use this form of organisation, but circulars and pamphlets that came out from the Ministry immediately after the war certainly encouraged LEAs to adopt tripartite structures. Consequently, during the 1940s and 1950s selective systems of secondary schooling became, with few minor exceptions, universal in this country.

In many areas of the country the so-called tripartite system was, in practice, bipartite. Aptitudes for technical subjects were almost impossible to identify at the age of 11, and secondary technicals proved more expensive to provide than grammar or secondary modern schools. As a result, a number of LEAs either did not set up such schools or phased them out after relatively brief experiments. There were often considerable disparities between localities in their relative provisions for grammar and modern places. In some LEAs as few as 10 per cent of the age group obtained grammar school places, but in some authorities in Wales over 40 per cent went to such schools. These inequalities were the result of local educational traditions and conditions, and it was difficult to find a rationale for such disparity within the national education service.

During the late 1940s there was enthusiasm for the new secondary modern schools, and teachers with 'pioneering spirit' often took up posts in these institutions. For some years HMI took the view that secondary modern schools should be kept free from the pressures and constraints of external examinations and in the early 1950s secondary moderns were officially discouraged from offering General Certificate of Education (GCE) courses to even their most able pupils. Later even those with the greatest faith in the accuracy of 11+ selection tests had to acknowledge that there was considerable overlap in ability between some pupils in grammar and modern schools, and further parental and teacher pressure led to a change in policy. By the early 1960s GCE courses in the top classes of secondary modern schools were far from uncommon.

From 1944 the Ministry and the LEAs tried to ensure that there was 'parity of esteem' between the different kinds of secondary schools. The public, particularly parents, remained unconvinced. They felt that the grammar schools took a disproportionate share of resources, and they observed how grammar schools kept their pupils longer and provided the main route to higher education and white-collar occupations. Many members of the public persisted in regarding the grammar schools as the only 'genuine' secondary schools and saw the secondary moderns as renamed senior elementary schools. Lower middle-class parents, sometimes in professional or semi-professional occupations, became very concerned if their children failed to obtain grammar school places. They were acutely aware of the relative status of the secondary schools in their neighbourhoods, and the dissatisfaction of a proportion of this social group with the results of selection at 11 was not unimportant in the demise of the tripartite system in certain solid surburban districts.

Selection at eleven became a veritable industry in its own right during the 1940s and 1950s. The confidence in intelligence tests to identify innate ability which remained almost static throughout life was unshaken in the early years. There can be little doubt that the strong emphasis on preparation for the crucially important 11+ tests caused anxiety amongst children and parents and had detrimental restricting effects on the teaching methods and curriculum of junior schools in this period. By the late 1950s psychologists had produced considerable evidence which cast doubts upon the selection procedures. At about the same time sociologists had shown that in reality the tripartite system was based on social selection with class background an important determinant of success or failure at school. By the end of this decade some educationists and administrators had lost their faith in selection and the prevailing divisions in secondary education.

From the early post-war years multilateral or comprehensive schools had been established in a few widely scattered areas of the country. In a rural district such as Anglesey, for example, it was felt unnecessary to develop separate small grammar and modern schools just to keep them apart and comprehensives emerged. Large new housing estates were sometimes similarly provided with comprehensives. A number of LEAs – including London, Middlesex, Coventry and parts of the West Riding – showed interest in experimenting with comprehensives. One of the common arguments used against comprehensive schools in this period was that the schools needed to be extremely large to generate viable sixth-form numbers. As the proportion of young people staying on in the sixth form increased dramatically in the 1950s, this point lost much of its validity. It was also pointed out that some of the leading public and direct grant grammar schools were large and few saw disadvantages in their size.

During the 1950s the question of secondary school organisation became increasingly politicised. In the 1940s leaders of the Labour Party had accepted the tripartite system although certain groups within this party had always favoured multilaterals or comprehensives. By the mid-1950s the abolition of selection at 11 became Labour Party policy. In contrast the Conservatives began to champion the cause of the grammar schools. Bitter disputes were fought out on party lines when the existence of certain grammar schools was threatened. Although, in general, the Conservative governments of the late 1950s and early 1960s wanted to retain the existing tripartite structure, Edward Boyle, who served as Minister of Education, appreciated that in some circumstances comprehensive schools had advantages and he encouraged members of his own party to accept them more readily.[10] By 1963 a majority of LEAs was working on schemes for at least some comprehensive schools, and in the Education Act of 1964 Boyle, prompted by Alec Clegg of the West Riding, encouraged further moves in this direction. In future, LEAs were enabled to transfer pupils from one stage of education to the other at ages other than 11. This made the development of middle schools possible, and patterns of school reorganisation such as 5–8 or 5–9 first schools; 8–12 or 9–13 middle schools; and 12–18 or 13–18 high schools were eventually taken up by a significant number of LEAs. By reorganising on three-tier lines, pupils could often be fitted into existing buildings more easily. Some educationists also believed that extending the best methods and approaches of the primary schools into the middle schools was liberating for the children, keeping them free from the pressures of external examinations for longer. During the 1970s middle schools emerged as an important force in the educational provision of certain areas of the country, but the demographic trends of the 1980s coupled, in some instances, with a desire to reorganise again on rather different principles, are now leading to their demise in a number of LEAs.

The Labour Government elected in 1964 set out its policy on secondary reorganisation in Circular 10/65.[11] Its declared aims were to end selection at eleven and to introduce comprehensive schools throughout the country. LEAs were asked to prepare and submit plans for reorganisation to the Secretary of State for approval. A number of acceptable forms of reorganisation (including 11–18 comprehensives; 11–16 comprehensives with sixth-form colleges; and middle school schemes) were included in the circular. In the next few years the majority of LEAs put forward their proposals and many of the schemes had been approved before Labour left office in 1970. One of Margaret Thatcher's first actions as the new Conservative Secretary of State was to issue Circular 10/70[12] which, in effect, cancelled the requirements of 10/65. By this time comprehensivisation had become highly charged and highly politicised. When Labour returned to power it eventually resorted to legislation in the Education Act of 1976 to goad the remaining LEAs into action on secondary reorganisation. In turn in the Education Act of 1979 the Conservatives repealed the sections of the 1976 Act relating to comprehensivisation. By the mid-1980s, excluding the independent sector, the vast majority of children of secondary age attended comprehensive schools, but about 10 per cent of the total were still accommodated in LEA grammar and secondary modern schools.

Primary education has changed profoundly since 1944. During the war the junior schools were aptly described as the

'Cinderellas' of the education service. Concepts of primary education were only just beginning to replace older notions of elementary schooling. Although they were often in nineteenth-century buildings and experiencing teacher shortages, primary schools began to experiment with more modern approaches to learning despite their large classes. As has been mentioned, primary schools were further constrained for twenty years or more by the need to prepare their older pupils for eleven-plus selection tests. Nonetheless, progress was made, and yet it did not stem from structural or administrative changes. It was not the Ministry, the DES or the LEAs that were responsible for the new developments, but teachers, heads and advisers. Their work received official encouragement in the Plowden Report[13] of 1967, but in some ways it was not until the late 1960s and 1970s that the primary schools ceased to be the 'Cinderellas' of the service. Lively debates about progressive approaches and methods in primary schools, of course, continue. There are few, however, currently working in the education service who would wish to return to the conditions and practices of the 1930s and 1940s. Yet it still remains a moot point whether the spectre of nineteenth-century elementary education has been completely laid to rest in this country, even in the last quarter of the twentieth.

REFERENCES

1. P. H. J. H. Gosden, 1966 *The Development of Educational Administration in England and Wales*, Blackwell, p. 2.
2. K. Evans, 1985 *The Development and Structure of the English School System*, Hodder and Stoughton, p. 30.
3. E. G. West, 1965 *Education and the State*, Institute of Economic Affairs and E. G. West, 1975 *Education and the Industrial Revolution*, Batsford.
4. P. H. J. H. Gosden, op. cit, p.129, quoting W. E. Forster.
5. R. H. Tawney, 1923 *Secondary Education for All*.
6. Board of Education, 1926 *The Education of the Adolescent* (Report of Consultative Committee on Education, Chairman Sir W. H. Hadow).
7. Board of Education, 1938 *Secondary Education with special reference to Grammar Schools and Technical High Schools* (Report of Consultative Committee on Education, Chairman W. Spens).
8. P. H. J. H. Gosden, 1976 *Education in the Second World War*, Chapter 11.
9. Secondary Schools Examinations Council, 1943 *Curriculum and Examinations in Secondary Schools* (Report of Committee, Chairman Sir C. Norwood,).
10. Lord E. Boyle, 1972 'The Politics of Secondary School Reorganisation: some Reflections', *Journal of Educational Administration and History*, Volume IV, No. 2 (June), pp. 28–38.

11. DES, 1965 Circular 10/65, *The Organisation of Secondary Education*, HMSO.
12. DES, 1970 Circular 10/70, *The Organisation of Secondary Education*, HMSO.
13. Central Advisory Council for Education, 1967 *Children and their Primary Schools* (Report of Committee, Chair Lady B. Plowden,).

FURTHER READING

Evans, K. 1985 *The Development and Structure of the English School System*, Hodder and Stoughton.
Gosden, P. H. J. H. 1966 *The Development of Educational Administration in England and Wales*, Blackwell.
Gosden, P. H. J. H. 1983 *The Education System since 1944*, Martin Robertson.
Lawson, J. and Silver, H. 1973 *A Social History of Education in England*, Methuen.
Lowe, R. 1988 *Education in the Post-war Years*, Routledge.
Sanderson, M. 1987 *Educational Opportunity*, Faber and Faber.

CHAPTER 2

Educational developments in the 1970s and 1980s

The 1972 Local Government Act, which will be considered more thoroughly in Chapter 4, brought into being on 1 April 1974 a new system of local government in England and Wales (outside the area of the now defunct Greater London Council). This date is also seen by many commentators on the educational scene as being the one in which the control of education began to slip away from the Local Education Authorities (LEAs) in two directions. On the one hand to the DES and on the other to the governing bodies of individual schools. The reasons for these changes are generally seen to be three-fold: demographic decline, public expenditure reductions and a public disillusionment with the education service replacing the optimism which had encouraged its expansion during the 1950s and 1960s.

The position of the DES was a strange one in that Section 1 of the 1944 Education Act had given the Secretary of State the 'catch all' power to 'secure the effective execution by Local Authorities under his control and direction of the national policy for providing a varied and comprehensive educational service in every area'. This power had hardly been used by successive Ministers and Secretaries of State. However in the mid-70s the civil servants of the Department drew up a document which became known as the Yellow Book, setting out their dissatisfaction with the way education was being provided. A summary of this unpublished book was leaked to Prime Minister James Callaghan who used it in a speech at Ruskin College, Oxford, in the autumn of 1976 and in doing so inaugurated a discussion on education which became known as the 'Great Debate'. One of the issues that was raised was the seeming inability of local government to agree (in the way that it had through the Association of Education Committees (AECs)) on common policies for education. The increasing reorganisation of secondary education along comprehensive lines had led to a polarisation within local government with the Labour-controlled authorities being committed to the reorganisation of their secondary schools as quickly as they could, while the Conservative-controlled authorities moved more slowly, or in some cases not at all. The 1976 Education Act, which made comprehensive reorganisation compulsory, was speedily repealed by the incoming Conservative administration in 1979. Another factor in the Great Debate was the increase in demand by parents and educational professionals for greater participation in education decision-making. These various factors led to the losing of power by the LEAs in the 1970s and 1980s. The first formal sign of this was the setting up of an independent enquiry into the management and government of schools in England and Wales. The committee was chaired by Tom Taylor (Chairman of Education in Blackburn County Borough) and this report became known as the Taylor Report. Its brief was to 'review the arrangements for the management and government of maintained primary and secondary schools in England and Wales, including the composition and functions of bodies of managers and governors, and their relationships with LEAs, with head teachers and staff of schools, with parents of pupils and with the local community at large; and to make recommendations.'

As well as the factors that have been already discussed, a study of managing and governing bodies between 1965 and 1969 (but not published until after 1974)[1] had found considerable dissatisfaction with the way many of these bodies were operating. Many schools did not have individual governing bodies but were grouped together with a number of other schools. Whilst the 1944 Act allowed this, it did not envisage groups as large as they had become. The effect of these groupings was that the managing or governing body simply 'rubber-stamped' decisions taken by the LEA. A high proportion were also dominated by councillors reflecting the political majority of the local council. Indeed, in some county boroughs up to 1974, *all* (except voluntary) schools were grouped together in a primary school managing body and a secondary school governing body.

The Taylor Report concluded that each school required its own governing body (the term to be used for both primary and secondary schools) which should be part of a continuum of responsibility from the LEA to the head of the school. Whilst the 1944 Act left the composition of managing and governing bodies to the LEAs, the Taylor Report recommended equal representation from four groups: the LEA; the school staff; the parents (and pupils); and the local community. It went on to say how responsibility for the curriculum, finance, staff appointments, admissions, suspensions and expulsions and school premises were to be divided between the governors and the LEA.

A 'note of extension' brought forward by a third of the members suggested that parents should have the legal right to be given information about the school that their child attended or intended to attend, should have consultations with teachers and should have the right of access to information about their child's education.

The Taylor Report found that changes were taking place in the management and government of schools, but the 'William Tyndale'* public enquiry showed that there were still problems with managing bodies. Some of the recommendations drew strong opposition from various sources: some of the LEAs did not like the concept of four equal partners; the NUT found the report a 'busybody's charter'; and the extension of governors' powers was disliked by teachers' unions and educational administrators.

Because of this opposition Shirley Williams, the then Secretary of State, divided the two issues of composition and power. The Government published a new Education Bill in 1978 which contained five clauses concerning school government. All schools were to have governing bodies and the Secretary of State was to make regulations about the size and membership of governing bodies in county and in voluntary schools. Governing bodies were to include representatives of parents, teachers and for county secondary schools the local community and pupil governors over the age of 16 (the legal implications of this latter proposal were ignored). Local authorities that wished to group schools had to obtain the Secretary of State's approval and all grouped schools were entitled to have parent and teacher representations on the governing bodies.

At the same time a White Paper, *The Composition of Governing Bodies* (Cmnd 7430 – December 1978),[2] set out the proposals for what was to be included in the Regulations, but it did not include recommendations on the powers of governors.

However the Bill never became an Act; it was still at the committee stage when the May 1979 election brought a change of government. Whilst the incoming government's first educational priority was to repeal the 1976 Education Act by passing the 1979 Education Act, it quickly published a Bill that was to become the 1980 Education Act. This included five clauses that were very similar to the clauses of the 1978 Bill. This Act contained many features other than changes in the composition of governing bodies, most importantly the sections concerned with school admissions and parental preferences, both areas which were discussed in the Taylor Report.

THE EDUCATION ACT 1980

The 1980 Education Act is one of four major pieces of educational legislation passed by the Conservative administrations of Margaret Thatcher between 1979 and 1988. As well as the two

---

* Problems arose at William Tyndale Junior School in London which led to the ILEA setting up a public enquiry by Robin Auld QC. One of the conclusions was that there were inadequacies in the system of managing the school.

areas already mentioned, it concerned itself with procedures for establishing new schools and closing old ones. It also introduced a new system of assisted places at independent schools; removed compulsion on local authorities to provide school meals; defined the local authorities' powers regarding nursery schools and made the payment of recoupment* automatic.

The clauses concerning school government changed the nomenclature for primary schools as recommended by the Taylor Report. It laid down that there must be parent and teacher governors on each governing body and that each school was to have its own governing body unless the LEA felt that two schools could share a governing body. There was no other legislation on the composition of governing bodies except for ensuring that there was a minor authority† representative on a primary school governing body where there was such an authority. It also simplified the majority held by the governors of an aided or special agreement school.

The implementation of many of the sections on governors did not formally take effect until 1 September 1985 although many LEAs had already done so before that date. There is no reference in the Act to the power of the governing body.

Sections 6 to 9 of the Act are entitled 'Admission to Schools' and were referred to in 1980 as a 'Parents' charter'. Parents already had certain rights to have their children educated according to their wishes under Section 76 of the 1944 Act and in the case of a dispute with their LEA had the right of appeal to the Secretary of State. In the mid- to late-1970s the Government was embarrassed by the large number of such appeals. Research has shown that it was not the parents as a whole who wanted choice, but that individual parents wanted access to the schools they preferred.[3] Section 6 of the 1980 Act gave parents this access, subject to their wishes being compatible with efficiency and economy. The section also applied to voluntary schools and allowed parents to choose a school in another LEA. Section 7 took parental choice further than before by giving them the right of appeal to a legally constituted local appeals panel. This was not as altruistic as it might seem at first sight. Some parents had been obtaining the schools of their choice by using the provisions of

---

* Recoupment is the payment by one LEA to another LEA of the costs of educating one of its children. This legislation was made necessary as a result of Section 6 of this Act.

† Minor authority: The district or parish council in a Shire county. The successor parish council in a metropolitan district. This representation goes back to the 1944 Act and the loss of educational powers to the county councils and county boroughs by the minor authority.

Section 37 of the 1944 Act. Under that section, if they kept their child away from school, a school attendance order was issued; and also under that section, parents were allowed to stipulate the school that was to be named in the school attendance order. The Secretary of State could then only refuse to name the school desired by the parent if it could be shown that the admission of one child to that school would give rise to unreasonable public expenditure. Thus parents who were prepared to sacrifice their child's education for a short period could gain the school of their choice while parents who were not prepared to go so far were not able to. Sections 10 and 11 of the 1980 Act made this procedure impossible and made school attendance orders subject to Section 7 of the Act, thus making all parents go through the same procedures. Schedule 2 of the Act laid down the constitution of the Appeals Committee and the procedures to be followed. These have both been reviewed since the Act came into effect and have only been revised very slightly. The Appeals Committee consists of three, five or seven people, comprising both members of the Authority or the Education Committee and other persons who have experience in education or parents of registered pupils at a school. The former category is not to outnumber the latter by more than one. People who have been involved in the decision at any stage are barred from membership and the Chairman of the Appeals Committee cannot be a member of the Education Committee.

Parents have to appeal in writing and are then allowed to appear before the Appeals Committee. They may be allowed 'to be accompanied by a friend or representative'[4], which means that they can have a solicitor to represent them if the authority agrees. The parents and the LEA both put their case and the Committee then has to make its decision, taking into account the preference expressed by the parents and the LEA's or governor's admission procedures. A simple majority is all that is required, and there is no appeal against the decision of the Committee.

To help parents make up their minds about choosing schools, Section 8 required LEAs and governors of aided schools to publish information about the rules governing admission to schools, the arrangements for parents to express a preference and the appeals procedures. In addition, they must give information about the number of places available and the age groups in which pupils are normally admitted. Circular 1/81 suggested that they should also give details of transport arrangements or assistance with transport costs. Since the Act was passed the Secretary of State has issued certain regulations which require parents to be issued with information on individual schools detailing, among other things, the rules of the school, the school's view on sex education, the curriculum and the school's view on punishment.

Having given parents the right to choose their child's school, within reasonable limits, the next sections of the Act legislated on how new schools were to be established, existing schools discontinued or have their size altered. As was seen in the previous chapter, central government theoretically had control of school building through the LEA's development plans and the use of Section 13 of the 1944 Act. Sections 12 to 16 of the 1980 Act revised the procedures and also had a new procedure for reducing school intakes (without closing any of the school buildings).

Section 13 of the 1944 Act required the Secretary of State's approval on all submissions to build, close or alter the size of the school. Section 12 of the 1980 Act revised this and, for county schools only, allowed the LEA to proceed with its proposals if there were no objections, unless the Secretary of State felt that there was a special reason for 'calling in' the proposals. This might happen if an LEA had attempted to close the school once and failed, and at the second attempt received no objections to their proposals. This could happen if a school had become so small that even the parents in the area realised that it was not viable. However, having turned down the closure proposals the first time, the Secretary of State might feel duty bound to consider the new case carefully. The Act required LEAs to be more specific than in the past on how they intended to implement their proposals. In addition, two very detailed circulars were issued advising LEAs on how they should consult with the public both before and after publishing the proposals. This advice appears to have lengthened the amount of time it takes an LEA to publish a Section 12 Notice. At the same time that LEAs had to undertake additional consultation, especially over school closures, they had been asked by successive Secretaries of State to take surplus places out of use. Sometimes the request and the Secretary of State's decisions have been in conflict. The Act, however, helped LEAs to take out of use spare school places where this did not involve a closure of the school. Under Section 15 an LEA can reduce the intake of a school by up to 20 per cent on what is known as the standard number. This, according to the Act, is the number in September 1979 in any age group that was admitted to a specific school. Whilst allowing the LEAs to take out spare places from under-subscribed schools, it also allowed them to limit the number of places available in popular schools in order to sustain numbers at less popular schools. This is because if a case came to appeal under this section, the Appeals Committee must base its decision on the number of admissions decided upon by the LEA and not on the number of children the school was originally built to house. This section has now been revised in the light of the 1988 Education Reform Act which, together with the 1986 Act, will be discussed later in this chapter.

Whether these sections of the Act have actually increased parental choice of school is open to debate and has been the subject of much research. The 1986 and 1988 Acts may eventually make parents more aware of their rights, and by providing more information on individual schools may help parents to make better choices about their children's schools.

Some parents were given a wider choice of school by Section 17 of the 1980 Act. This dealt with the Assisted Places Scheme which enabled children to attend independent schools, with the fees being remitted on an agreed scale related to parental income. LEAs play no part in this scheme. The schools involved deal directly with the DES.

Two other important aspects of this Act need to be looked at briefly. The first involves meals and milk, Section 22 removed from the LEAs the obligation to provide meals for children, except for children from very poor families. Section 23 is rather ironic as it restores the right – removed in 1971 by the then Secretary of State Margaret Thatcher (who was Prime Minister when this Act was passed) – for LEAs to provide milk for children over the age of eight. The other issue is that Section 24 makes the provision of nursery education only discretionary. There had been an unsettled debate on whether Section 8 of the 1944 Education Act had made it a duty (or only a power) for LEAs to provide for children under compulsory school age.

THE EDUCATION ACT 1981

Unusually, the 1979 to 1983 Conservative administration introduced two pieces of educational legislation relatively quickly. The 1980 Education Act was followed by one in the next year whose sole concern was that of special education. The 1944 Education Act had laid down how children with special educational needs were provided for, and the 1970 Education (Handicapped Children) Act had transferred the responsibility for severely mentally handicapped children's education to the LEAs from the Department of Health and Social Security. Children, however, were still originally categorised according to their major handicap. In 1974 Margaret Thatcher had established a committee under Lady Warnock to consider the whole question of special education. Section 10 of the 1976 Education Act stated that children with special needs should, wherever possible, be educated in normal schools, but this section was never implemented owing to the fact that the Warnock Report was due to be published. It was published in May 1978 and after the change of government in 1979 a White Paper was published in May 1980, a Bill was laid before Parliament in January 1981 and the Act received the Royal Assent in October of the same year. A remarkably speedy process for educational legislation resulting from such a report.

The Act is not very long but it contains many important rights for children with special educational needs. The first section defines special needs and introduces the term 'learning difficulty'. It states that a child has a learning difficulty if: '(a) He/She has a significantly greater difficulty in learning than the majority of children of his/her age; or (b) has a disability which either prevents or hinders him/her from making use of educational facilities of a kind generally provided in schools, within the area of the Local Authority concerned, for children of his/her age or (c)is under 5 and could fall into either of these categories if special provision is not made.' It does, however, specifically exclude children who have difficulties because the language in which they are taught is different from the one which at any time has been spoken at home. Section 2 then goes on to state that 'it shall be the duty of the Authority, if the conditions mentioned below are satisfied, to secure that he/she is educated in an ordinary school'. The conditions stated below are 'that account has been taken, in accordance with Section 7 of the views of the child's parents and that educating the child in an ordinary school is compatible with:(a) his/her receiving the special educational provision that he/she requires; (b) the provision of efficient education for the children with whom he/she will be educated; and (c) the efficient use of resources.'[5]

The Act then goes on to lay down the duties of an LEA to identify and assess a child who may have special educational needs and the way in which the LEAs should carry out the procedures to do so. If the LEA identifies a child as having a special educational need, then Section 7 gives very detailed instructions on how the LEA makes a statement on such a child, including the discussions which must take place with parents at every stage of the process. The LEA must seek medical, psychological, educational and such other advice as may be prescribed. During the making of the statement, discussions with the parent(s) may cause it to be modified at any stage before it is agreed. If the parents fail to agree with the statement, the LEA may still make it but the parent(s) then have the right to appeal to an Appeals Committee constituted in the same way as for the 1980 Act appeals. The Appeals Committee has the right to confirm the special education provision specified in the statement or to refer the case to the LEA for reconsideration in the light of the Committee's observation. If the parents are still not satisfied then there is the right of appeal to the Secretary of State. The Secretary of State has the right to have the child re-examined and to consult the LEA. Having done so, three options are then open:

(a) to confirm the special education provision specified in the statement; (b) to amend the statement as far as it specifies the special educational provision and make other such consequential amendments to the statement as considered appropriate; or (c) to direct the LEA to cease to maintain the statement.

The Act deals with a number of other matters such as the duties of Health Authorities, the opening and closing of special schools and the approval of special schools (both maintained and independent). Its major facets are those that have been considered: the definitions of 'special educational needs' and 'learning difficulties'; the right to integration wherever possible; and the making of a statement. The Act also goes further than any previous legislation in the rights it confers on parents, but strangely enough it does not give the child any specific rights. However the DES in Circular 1/83 gave guidance to LEAs that 'the feelings and perceptions of the child concerned should be taken into account, and the concept of partnership should, whenever possible, be extended to older children and young people'.

The White Paper of 1980 contained the words 'only when the economic situation improves sufficiently will it be possible to bring to fruition all the committed efforts of those engaged in meeting special educational needs'. Yet seven months later the preamble to the Bill stated 'the Bill revises the statutory basis for arrangements which already exist in most areas for the educational provision for children with special educational needs. . . and should not give rise to significant additional expenditure'. The extension of the arrangements for parental appeals '. . . should not significantly increase the cost of these arrangements'.[6] This proved not to be the case and the lack of additional resources meant that many LEAs did not fulfill the main principles of the Act. In February 1987 the Commons Select Committee on Education opened an enquiry into the implementation of the Act. When this reported in 1988 it proved that in many cases children with special educational needs were either not being integrated or were, in fact, not receiving the facilities required under the Act.

THE EDUCATION (NO 2) ACT 1986

It was 1986 before the next piece of educational legislation was passed. Yet the intervening period saw intense discussion on the education service. This period was also marked by large-scale industrial action by schoolteachers over their pay, which was complicated by the fact that the Government (as the paymasters, not the employers) wanted to see the pay settlement tied to conditions of service. Standards in education were being questioned throughout this period and there is a need to consider several

Green and White Papers before turning to the 1986 Education Act.

In 1983 a White Paper entitled 'Teaching Quality' was published. This paper made a range of points specifically directed to the practice of teaching and the process of professionalisation. It called for a better match between teachers' qualifications and the subjects they taught. It then went on to discuss how initial teacher training could be improved. It also raised the question of appraisal and professional development amongst teachers, including the need for more in-service training which in turn led in 1987 to a restructuring of the financial arrangements for such training.

Many of the ideas in this White Paper were reiterated in the 1984 White Paper 'Better Schools'. This was the forerunner to the 1986 Education Act and included some of the points from a Green Paper 'Parental Influence at School' also published in that year. This latter document, which suggested that parents should form the majority on school governing bodies, met with almost total opposition from the different sectors of the educational world. However, it contained many other ideas on the curriculum, on staffing, on reports to parents and on finance which were to find their way not only into 'Better Schools' but also into the 1986 Education Act.

These papers, together with other central government pronouncements and the withdrawal of central government finance from local government, marked a period in the first half of the 80s when the balance of power in the control of education was subtly moved from the LEAs to central government and to individual school governing bodies. The abolition of the independent Schools Council in 1983 and its replacement by two government controlled bodies, the Secondary Examination Council and the Schools Curriculum Development Committee, put curriculum control very firmly in the hands of central government and was the first move towards a National Curriculum. This, as will be seen later, reached its fulfilment in the abolition of these latter two bodies and the establishment of new ones as a result of the Education Reform Act 1988.

The 1986 Education Act went through Parliament at a time when the education service, certainly as far as primary and secondary schools were concerned, was in turmoil. Both central government (the real paymasters) and the local authorities (the actual employers) were agreed that there needed to be a pay agreement linked to a conditions of service agreement. The schoolteachers were very reluctant to do so, as their conditions of service were so loosely defined that they were able to disrupt the education of children at very little cost to themselves by withdrawing goodwill over meal supervision, out-of-school activities (including parents' meetings) and most importantly by refusing to cover for absent colleagues. For a long period in the mid-1980s, few school children enjoyed a normal school life, and in the midst of this the Government passed an Education Act which profoundly affected the control of schools and more importantly what went on in them.

The Act concerned itself with two major areas: school government and the organisation of the functions of schools. Within these two areas, especially the latter, it dealt with some extremely important issues. In a Miscellaneous chapter it also abolished corporal punishment, allowed for the appraisal of teacher's performance, concerned itself with the freedom of speech and political indoctrination, and allowed students in further education access to courses in other LEAs. It will be necessary to consider many of these issues further, but first let us look at the area of school government.

As has been seen, the concept of parental control put forward in 'Parental Influence at School' had been modified in 'Better Schools' and the suggestions put forward in the White Paper were those which became law. They owe much to the recommendations of the 1979 Taylor Report on Governing Bodies.

The Act reduced the dominance of the LEAs on governing bodies and distributed the places on them almost equally between parents, LEA representatives, teaching staff, including the head teacher (if that individual so desired), and representatives of the local community. In order to ensure that the governing bodies functioned effectively the Act took fifteen sections to spell out how governing bodies were to be set up and run before going on to consider organisation and function. Here the Act laid down that the general responsibility for the conduct of schools was placed with the governors. It then laid down how the school curriculum was to be agreed between the LEA, the governors and head teacher and how parents were to be informed about such decisions. The Act then gave detailed instructions about the disciplining of pupils, especially concerning the exclusion from school of individual pupils.

A very short section of the Act concerned finance. This was in line with the thinking of a number of LEAs who in the late 1970s and early 1980s were beginning to delegate considerable financial control to individual schools. This was one kind of accountability that the Act called for; another was the requirement of the governors and head teacher to produce annual reports and also to hold an annual parents' meeting. The parents' meeting was able, if it was quorate, to pass resolutions concerning the school, the governors and the LEA.

This part of the Act concluded with very detailed instructions on how staff, including heads, were to be appointed, and these sections were again part of the process of removing power from the LEA and putting it in the hands of the governing body. It was felt by many commentators at the time that several sections of the Act were a reaction to individual occurrences which had caused publicity or problems, or both. The matter of the appointment and dismissal of staff, it was felt, owed a great deal to the conflict between the City of Bradford LEA and Ray Honeyford, one of its head teachers, where the rights of the LEA and the governing body were disputed through to the appeal courts and only stayed out of the House of Lords when Honeyford took early retirement.* Equally, the long sections on disciplining pupils and exclusion owed much to the Poundswick case in Manchester where teachers withdrew their labour when the LEA instructed them to reinstate and teach pupils who had been excluded for allegedly writing libellous statements about staff on walls and blackboards around the school. The Act actually set up an Appeals Committee open equally to excluded pupils or to governors ordered by the LEA to readmit such pupils.

Some of the sections in the Miscellaneous chapter of the Act were included for similar reasons, though others were agreed because of rulings in other courts. In the latter category were the sections concerning corporal punishment and school transport; in the former were subsections such as those concerning 'freedom of speech in universities, colleges and polytechnics', 'political indoctrination' and 'sex education'. The freedom of speech section followed a series of incidents where politicians (usually of a Right-wing persuasion) were either forbidden entry to Seats of Learning by the student body or were not allowed to be heard once in the Institution. The political indoctrination and sex education sections are seen as a response of the Conservative Government to the actions of councils controlled by that section of the Labour Party popularly known at the time as the 'Loony Left'. It has already been mentioned that the time leading up to the 1986 Education Act was one which had seen teacher unrest over their pay and conditions of service. This issue will be considered in Chapter 5.

In this chapter we have looked mainly at the schools because post-school education will be considered in other chapters. It is perhaps worthwhile noting that the theme running through this chapter is one of power being taken from the LEAs and in some cases the DES. It can equally be applied in many cases both to schools and to the post-school educational world. Thus in 1987 a

---

* Ray Honeyford had been appointed to Drummond Middle School which had a large proportion of black pupils, many of whom were of the Islamic faith. He wrote a series of articles concerning multi-racial education which disagreed with the policy statement on this matter from his employing authority.

White Paper 'Higher Education, Meeting the Challenge' recommended the removal from local authority control of all the polytechnics together with the colleges of higher education which had more than 55 per cent of advanced work. This was 'implemented' in the 1988 Education Reform Act and came into effect from April 1989.

THE AUDIT COMMISSION

Before turning to the 1988 Education Reform Act, we need to consider the influence of the Audit Commission on the education service. The Audit Commission was established in 1983 as a result of the 1982 Local Government Finance Act. It is an independent body and its remit is 'The concentration of resources and effort on improvements that are achievable without any adverse effect on the level or quantity of the services to the public.'

The Audit Commission issued some fourteen reports between February 1984 and March 1986 of which three were concerned with education. It looked at 'Non-teaching costs in Secondary Schools'; 'Better Value in FE' and 'Better Management of Secondary Education'. In each of these reports the Commission made recommendations for action to LEAs and to central government. In 1986 the Commission published a handbook entitled 'Performance Review in Local Government' in which education was considered alongside six other local authority services. Within the Education Section the areas considered were nursery/primary, secondary, children with special needs, school meals and milk, higher and further education and ancillary services. A common pattern was followed in each area, first by a look at the current management issues, then a bibliography and finally a performance review guide. The booklet stated that the auditor's interest ensured that these issues had been addressed and that appropriate policies of management arrangements had been determined. It went on to say that it was not suggested that there should be a uniform approach to service outputs or standard levels of output, but rather authorities should make searching enquiries into why they differ from other authorities.

The Audit Commission's work had a mixed reception from the local authorities. There were some who saw it as a further example of the creeping trend to centralisation, whilst others saw its work as a useful management tool. The recommendations from the Audit Commission influenced policy-making at both local and central levels. Thus the FE report asked why senior lecturers spent less time teaching than their less experienced colleagues. In the subsequent negotiations on FE lecturers' pay and conditions of service, the employers' side, with support from the DES, changed considerably the class contact arrangements for FE lecturers.

Equally, the report on the management of secondary schools contains the recommendation: 'delegate as much responsibility as possible to heads and governing bodies, together with the authority necessary to discharge it.' This became a major element of the 1988 Education Reform Act.

THE EDUCATION REFORM ACT 1988

We now turn to the 1988 Education Reform Act which is the largest piece of educational legislation since 1944, and whilst it does not take the place of that legislation as being the Act forming the legal basis of the education system in England and Wales, it amends it by totally altering the relationship between central and local government and the schools.

The 1988 Education Reform Act changed the basic power structure within the education service. It increased central government's control of the system by spelling out the powers of the Secretary of State but it did not repeal the 'catch all' power given in Section 1 of the 1944 Act. At the same time it also took powers away from the LEAs and gave those powers to the schools and colleges, mainly through increasing the authority of governing bodies. It removed the polytechnics and colleges of higher education from local authority control, and by establishing new funding arrangements made them more accountable to central government. It also altered the funding arrangements for the universities. Yet, perhaps the reform which caused the most comment was the introduction of the National Curriculum, and in this it provided a strange paradox with those parts of the Act which gave schools freedom to react to market forces. Whilst the Act allows, indeed encourages, schools to opt out of the local government system, to enrol pupils up to numbers agreed a decade ago and, by controlling their own finances, to respond to the demands of the market place, it then imposes what should be taught for the vast majority of the time.

Let us consider the Act by dividing it into eight divisions. The Act itself actually has three parts with several chapters and 238 sections. The divisions we shall consider are (i) the National Curriculum and Assessment, (ii) Open enrolment, (iii) Finance and staff, (iv) Grant Maintained schools, (v) Higher and further education, (vi) the Finance and government of locally funded further and higher education, (vii) Education in Inner London and (viii) Miscellaneous provisions of the Act.

(i) The National Curriculum and Assessment

The National Curriculum has three core subjects and seven foundation subjects. The core subjects are English, Mathematics and Science; the foundation ones are History, Geography, Technology, Music, Art, Physical Education and (at the secondary stage) a foreign language. (Welsh is a core subject in Welsh-speaking schools and a foundation subject in other schools in Wales.) Religious Education is included for all pupils – especially those staying on beyond the statutory school age. The arrangements for Religious Education are far more complex than those in the 1944 Act, putting the emphasis on the Christian aspect of both worship and teaching, unless schools are exempted by the local Standing Advisory Council on Religious Education.

Section 2 states that the curriculum shall specify in relation to each of the core and foundation subjects:

(a) The knowledge, skills and understanding that pupils of different abilities and maturities are expected to have by the end of each key stage. (Attainment targets.)

(b) The matters, skills and processes that are required to be taught to pupils of different abilities and maturities during each key stage. (Programmes of study.)

(c) The arrangements for assessing pupils at or near the end of each key stage for the purpose of ascertaining what they have achieved in relation to the attainment targets for that stage. (Assessment arrangements.)

The end of each key stage is by the ages of 7, 11, 14 and 16.

Most of the details for the implementation of this part of the Act will be carried out by the issuing of orders. These Statutory Instruments will be laid before Parliament before becoming law. The original list of core and foundation subjects can be amended by order. A duty is placed on both the LEA and school governors to ensure that the National Curriculum is implemented. Jointly in the case of local authority schools and by the governors alone in the case of Aided and Grant Maintained Schools.

The Act does not lay down any periods of time for which the compulsory parts of the curriculum should be taught. Indeed an amendment to the Bill, Section 4(3), states that the establishment of the National Curriculum by order may not require '(a) that any particular period or periods of time should be allocated during any key stages to the teaching of any programmes of study or any matter, skill or process forming part of it; or (b) that provision of any particular kind should be made in school timetables for the periods to be allocated to such teaching during any stage.' Nevertheless, the Secretary of State, Mr Baker stated at the time of the second reading of the Bill that he did not think it would take less than 70 per cent of school time. An earlier DES consultative paper had suggested 75 to 85 per cent. Only the application of the orders will determine how much time is needed.

(ii) Open enrolment

Whilst the 1980 Education Act gave parents increased rights over admissions to school it also allowed LEAs to artificially fix the number of children allowed to enter a school. The 1988 legislation reverts to the standard number using the 1979 entry to schools as a base line. There are arrangements for the governors of Aided or Special Agreement schools to be able to disregard the standard number, if admitting non-denominational children up to the standard number would alter the character of the school, or involve them in additional expense by keeping more of the school open than was necessary. Section 30 of the Act is concerned with this matter.

(iii) Finance and staff

This chapter of the Act looks at financial delegation, though the terms local financial management and local management of schools are used variously outside the legislation. Local authorities are required by the Act to prepare schemes of financial delegation for all secondary schools and primary schools of over 200 pupils (though the Secretary of State may by order lower this number). Delegation of finance is described in great detail in DES Circular No. 7/88 but is based primarily on a weighted per capita formula. The governing bodies are responsible for controlling the budgets. Similarly the staffing matters in this chapter are there to give the governors control over appointments and dismissals so that they can better manage their schools.

Not all the finances have to be delegated to a school. There are headings which must be excluded, such as capital expenditure, debt charges and the items covered by specific central government grant. In addition the Secretary of State may, under Section 38(4)(d), exclude other areas. At the time of writing, central administration, inspectors/advisers and home–school transport had been excluded. Circular 7/88 laid down other items which the LEA had discretion to exclude. These included school meals, educational psychology service, education welfare, statement of pupils and special units, peripatetic and advisory teachers, structural maintenance and repairs, pupil support, and certain staff costs including safeguarding and cover. However, these discretionary exclusions must not be more than 10 per cent of the budget and this is to reduce to 7 per cent by 1991. The Act states that finance must be allocated by means of a formula, common to all schools after certain transitory arrangements, and must also be applied to schools which do not, as yet, have delegated finance.

Once a school has a delegated budget the governing body has the power to select a person for appointment or to require that any person should cease to work at the school. The LEA, subject to certain safeguards, must appoint the person recommended by the governors. They also must dismiss on the governors' recommendation unless the person is not employed by the LEA to work solely at the school. (Many teachers were appointed to the service of the LEA, and not to a particular school, prior to the 1988 legislation.) Schedule 3 to the Act sets out how appointments and dismissals are to be carried out. The appointment of heads and deputies require the advice of the Chief Education Officer; for other appointments he/she may give advice if asked.

(iv) Grant maintained schools

Section 52 gives a legal basis for a new category of schools which the Secretary of State has 'a duty to maintain'. Again all secondary schools are eligible for this status but only primary schools with more than 300 on roll qualify. This minimum number can be revised or abolished by the Secretary of State at a future date.

The Act lays down who the governors of the new school will be, dividing them into categories of parents, teachers, head and 'first' governors. This latter category are the nominees of the existing governors in the case of a county school or the foundation governors from a voluntary school. 'First' governors must form the majority of the governing body. Once the school is established the Act gives details of how it is to be financed and run.

The procedure for acquiring grant maintained status which has become commonly known as 'opting out' is started by a ballot of parents. This is requested in one of two ways: firstly, by a simple majority of the governors at two meetings held not less than twenty-eight or more than forty-eight days apart; secondly, by a written demand signed by a number of parents of registered pupils at the school equal to at least 20 per cent of the number of registered pupils. The governors have to decide who is the parent of a registered child if there is any doubt. The Act lays down, in great detail, how the ballot is to be carried out and what information is to be given to the parents. If, when the ballot is held, more than 50 per cent of those enfranchised vote, then the result is by simple majority. If less than 50 per cent vote then a second ballot has to be held within fourteen days. Regardless of turnout, the majority decision on this ballot stands. If the result is in favour of opting out the governors have six months to publish their proposals and send a copy to the Secretary of State. (They must have informed the LEA and/or the trustees as soon as a decision to hold a ballot was held.) When the proposals are published objections can be made (as in the case of proposals under Section 12, etc., of the 1980 Act) by ten or more local government electors, the trustees, the governing body of any school affected by the proposals and any LEA concerned.

The Act also legislates for the financial arrangements by which the Secretary of State will pay a grant and also how recruitment will be made from the local authorities concerned. The formula referred to earlier for calculating financial delegation to LEA schools will serve as the basis for calculating the budget for a Grant Maintained school.

Grant Maintained schools will have to admit pupils up to their standard number, and in doing so they must not change the 'character' of the school without publishing notices under Section 12 and 13 of the 1980 Education Act. This means that, according to the law, a Grant Maintained school that has been a comprehensive school cannot skew it's intake and so become a grammar school by stealth.

The question of religious teaching in Grant Maintained schools is in line with the normal practice according to the agreed syllabus in all ex-county schools and ex-controlled schools (except where parents demand denominational teaching) and according to the provisions of the trustees in ex-Aided schools. To alter these arrangements a 'change of character' would have to be accepted. However, in ex-controlled schools the governors will be predominantly trustees. Sections 64(1)(d)(ii) and 64(2) make no distinction between the types of voluntary schools in constituting the initial governing body of a Grant Maintained school.

The law on Grant Maintained schools also allows for discontinuance either by the governors or by the Secretary of State who has to give seven years' notice of the intention to do so. However, where there is mismanagement the Secretary of State can appoint two extra governors.

Section 105 is concerned with the arrangements of the establishment of City Technology Colleges (CTCs) and of City Colleges for the Technology of the Arts (CCTAs). The Secretary of State had already agreed to the first of these before the Act was promulgated.

(v) Higher and further education

For the first time ever 'higher' education is defined. It had previously been simply part of further education. Section 121(2) defines the institutions which left local authority control, under this legislation. All those institutions whose full-time equivalent enrolments for courses of advanced further education exceeded 350 and also exceeded 55 per cent of its full-time equivalent enrolment numbers or its full-time equivalent enrolment numbers for such courses exceeded 2,500. This removed all the polytechnics and some twenty-five colleges from local authority control. Not only these institutions but also the colleges which already had voluntary Aided status were, in the terms of the Education Act, to be funded by the Polytechnics and Colleges Funding Council.

The Act set up two new bodies: the Polytechnics and Colleges Funding Council (PCFC) which replaced the National Advisory Body, and the Universities Funding Council (UFC) which replaced the Universities Grants· Committee. These bodies fund their respective parts of higher education. The bodies are both appointed by the Secretary of State and include people with academic experience and also with business experience. The UFC advises the Secretary of State and distributes funds to universities for education and research and providing facilities to do so. The PCFC has a similar role for its institutions.

Whilst the legislation does not appear in this section, the Act in its Miscellaneous section legislates on academic tenure and academic freedom. It establishes Commissioners to review and revise the statutes of universities and colleges to allow them to dismiss àcademics for reasons of redundancy or good cause. An amendment moved in the House of Lords protects academic freedom and prevents dismissal on the grounds of questioning received wisdom or expressing controversial or unpopular opinions.

These matters are discussed in more detail in Chapter 6.

(vi) Finance and government of locally funded further and higher education

The Act then moves on to give to the colleges left in the local authority sector the same kind of financial delegation that the schools have. This issue is also discussed in Chapter 6.

(vii) Education in Inner London

As was seen earlier, education in London from 1965 was the responsibility of the Outer London boroughs and the Inner London Education Authority (ILEA). This latter is the area covered by the twelve Inner London boroughs and the City of London, an area co-terminous with the original London School Board of

1870. It was formerly a Committee of the Greater London Council but after the abolition of that body it was directly elected. (It
therefore left the education scene in the same way as it entered
it – a single-purpose, directly elected body, unique amongst
LEAs.) The functions of the ILEA were transferred from 1 April
1990 to the twelve Inner London boroughs and the City of London.

It is not the purpose of this book to discuss the arguments over
the abolition of the ILEA, suffice it to say that what the 1988
Education Reform Act eventually achieved had been the subject
of debate since 1902.

(viii) Miscellaneous provisions

As with every major Education Act the opportunity was taken to
tidy up pieces of legislation which are required to be enacted for
a number of reasons. We have already seen that the Secretary of
State introduced legislation on CTCs even though he had the
power to set them up prior to this. The Act legislated on the
vexed question of charges in schools and allowed for charges to
be made for such matters as individual instrumental music tuition,
education outside school hours, the recovery of wasted examination fees and other 'permitted charges'.

The governing bodies were given powers to determine the
length and organisation of the school day, but must consult the
local authority and give notice of any changes (together with the
local authority's views) in the annual report to parents, whose
views they must consider. They must give three months' notice
of such changes, which can only be made at the start of the school
year. The local authority still has the duty to fix school terms.

Because of the likelihood of large-scale changes in ownership
or control for a great number of education institutions an Educational Assets Board has been set up to assist the Secretary of
State in such transfers.

The Act makes it a criminal offence to sell unrecognised
degrees or anything else which purports to confer the right· to an
academic title. The Act has towards its end a strange section concerning itself with British schools in Europe. These are not Her
Majesty's Forces schools but independent schools in the EEC.
Perhaps this is a clause preparing the way for 1992.

The Act will take many years to implement. Large sections
came into force on 29 July 1988; others are still to be implemented as this book goes to press, especially those concerned
with education in London.

REFERENCES

1. G. Baron and D. A. Howell 1974 *The Government and Management of Schools*, Athlone Press.
2. DES, 1978 *The Composition of Governing Bodies*, HMSO.
3. A. Stillman and K. Maychell, 1986 *Choosing Schools: Parents, LEAs and the 1980 Education Act*, NFER/Nelson.
4. The Education Act 1980, Schedule 2, Part II, s. 6, HMSO.
5. The Education Act 1981, HMSO.
6. H. C. Bill 48. 1981 *Education: A Bill to make provisions with respect to children with special educational needs*, HMSO, p. 3.

FURTHER READING

Fenwick, I. and McBride, P. 1982 *The Government of Education in Britain*, Martin Robertson.
Gosden, P. H. J. H. 1983 *The Education System since 1944*, Martin Robertsons.
MacClure, S. 1988 *Education Reformed*, Hodder and Stoughton.
Regan, D. 1984 *Local Government and Education*, Allen and Unwin.

CHAPTER 3

The role of central government in contemporary education administration

The major government department which concerns itself with education is the Department of Education and Science (DES) but since the end of the 1970s the Training Agency, (formerly called the Manpower Services Commission and, later, the Training Commission) together with the Department of Employment, have played increasingly larger parts. The Treasury, of course, concerns itself with all departments of State and its role will be considered in Chapter 5.

It is to the DES that we must first turn our attention. This is the collective name for all the staff who assist the Secretary of State for Education and Science in carrying out his/her function. We saw in Chapter 1 how the Department originated through its change in status from a Ministry in 1964. We also saw in the previous chapter that the last decade has seen the control of the education service move more and more to central government. It can be said that this was the original intention of the drafters of the 1944 Education Act when they included in the very first section of that Act the words 'it should be the duty of the Minister of Education (revised in 1964 to Secretary of State for Education and Science) . . . to secure the effective execution by local authorities, under his control and direction, of the national policy providing a varied and comprehensive educational service in every area.' (We need to remember that 'comprehensive' had not been used in the way it is now used to describe a particular type of secondary school.) This is a total change of central government policy because between its conception in 1899 and its replacement in 1944 the Board of Education had been purely regulatory. As a result of the 1944 Act the formulation of policy as well as the direction of its implementation lay with the central department of State. The diversities in educational provision which the Second World War had revealed – partly through the evacuation of children and partly through the mass testing of the male population on conscription – meant that in 1944 there was very little opposition to the new powers that were given to the centre. These new powers enabled great advances to be made, especially in the 1950s and 1960s in the areas of school building and secondary school examination. The provision of secondary school places for all children was a tremendous achievement in which central government played the major role, but it was assisted in its task by the cooperation of the LEAs mainly through their national body, the Association of Education Committees (AEC), which acted as a pressure group especially in times of economic crisis. The influence of the AEC began to wane once the consensus on the type of secondary school which should be provided began to break down in the late 1960s and early 1970s. Similarly with examinations and the curriculum, as we shall see later in the chapter, the influence of central government departments has differed greatly over the decades since 1944.

What then does the DES do and how great is its involvement in actually running the education service in England and Wales? The answer to the second part is, of course, that the majority of the day-to-day provision of education is in the hands of the LEAs, the schools (both maintained and independent) and the universities and institutes of higher education. The DES has very little responsibility. It is not a provider in any large part of the country's educational establishments. As a result of the Education Reform Act 1988 it now funds, in part, City Technology Colleges and meets the whole costs of Grant Maintained schools (although this money comes out of the Department of the Environment's block grant to the local authority in which the school is situated). Increasingly the DES makes policy statements in various forms which more and more are having an effect on service provision. Increasingly the statements involve the curriculum and they are disseminated through HMI and the National Curriculum Council (NCC). To this theme we shall return later, but first let us look at the Department of Education itself and in this we shall include Her Majesty's Inspectorate.

The DES is a very small government department mainly because of its non-executive role. In fact the 1944 Act gave the Minister very few specific powers. These included the power to issue regulations on such matters as school milk and meals, children requiring special educational provision, the standards for school premises and grants for educational services. The powers of the Secretary of State have been greatly increased as a result of the 1988 Education Reform Act. The Secretary of State lays regulations before Parliament for a period of forty days during which time they may be nullified by an adverse vote of either House. The Secretary of State also has other powers such as determining the number of teachers to be trained; administering their superannuation scheme (there is a separate branch of the Department based at Darlington specifically for this purpose); settling disputes within the education service and, since 1983, hearing appeals from parents whose children have special educational needs; and, perhaps one of the most important powers, forecasting a level of local authority expenditure on education which central government will need to fund.

To help the Secretary of State in these functions there are two Parliamentary Under-Secretaries of State and the civil servants of the Department who come under the Permanent Secretary. The Permanent Secretary has three Deputy Secretaries who are responsible for schools and educational buildings, further and higher education, together with science and teachers, external relations, educational research and statistics. In addition the Department has its own legal adviser, Accountant General and Director of Establishments. HMI, headed by the Senior Chief Inspector, works closely with the Department reporting on the state of education and advising ministers.

The work of the DES is divided into specific areas of concern, or sections, and, in turn, each section is subdivided into a number of branches. The simplest way to discover exactly what the DES does is to look briefly at the work of these sections and branches, and of the HMI. (In 1985 the Department published a document entitled *The DES – A Brief Guide*, in which fuller descriptions of each section and branch can be found.[1] Unfortunately this publication is now somewhat out of date and the only up-to-date information available about the structure of the DES is that taken from the various educational yearbooks. The information used here was correct at the end of 1988.) In looking at the work of the DES we shall begin with the section entitled 'Primary and Secondary Education – Educational Buildings'. Within it there are four main branches called Schools 1, Schools 2, School 3 and Architects and Buildings. Schools 1, which is divided into four divisions, is concerned with the organisation and supply of schools including relationships with individual LEAs. This branch tends to be organised on a divisional basis with officers in the branch having fairly close liaison with individual local authorities. The branch is also responsible for the organisation of schools including falling rolls and proposals under Sections 12 to 15 of the Education Act 1980. It is concerned with capital expenditure on education, with school admissions, with school governments, with independent schools and the Assisted Places Scheme. It is also concerned with the implementation of the Education Reform 1988 Act. Schools 2 looks after such matters as the educational aspect of urban programmes and policies for inner cities, education in a multi-ethnic society, education welfare services, behaviour of school children, educational provision for children with special educational needs, preparing young people for adult and working life, as well as international relations. Schools 3 is concerned almost wholly with the school curriculum, National Curriculum Council, Schools Examination and Assessment Council and this, of course, includes all the various aspects of the National Curriculum which are dealt with in different divisions of this branch. Examinations – GCSE, AS and 'A' level – and the machinery for testing and assessment at 7, 11, 14 and 16 together with records of achievement are dealt with by a fourth division of this branch. The Architects and Buildings branch is, as its name suggests, the branch concerned with the buildings of all kinds of educational establishments.

The second section we turn to is that entitled 'Further and Higher Education – Science'. This is divided into four branches. The first three are simply called Further and Higher Education branches 1, 2 and 3 and the fourth is a Science branch. Branch 1 is concerned with higher education within both the universities and the higher education institutions and has the responsibility for the polytechnics and colleges sector. It also oversees the Government's policy on overseas students. Further and Higher Education branch 2 is concerned with the finance, government and law of maintained FE, general policy on education and training of 16- to 19-year-olds, the youth service, the national council for Vocational Qualifications and such matters. Branch 3 looks very generally at the whole area of adult education and retraining including such projects as REPLAN and PICKUP. It also concerns itself with certain aspects of the government of universities and maintained sectors education and a further division within this branch looks at mandatory awards in England and Wales and student scholarships. The Science branch is responsible for the policy and funding for basic civil service science under the science budget and for the Advisory Board for Research Councils as well as for the Royal Society and various other scientific bodies.

The Finance branch of the DES has four divisions, the first concerned with public expenditure planning and parliamentary estimates as well as central government expenditure and local authority capital expenditure. The second division is involved with local authority expenditure (although of course the DES has no control over this). It concerns itself with supplying information to the Department of the Environment on local authorities' expenditure and forecasting, and rates support grant, pooling and educational support grants. The third division is simply an accounting branch for the Department itself while the fourth division is the internal audit division of the Department.

The Department of Education has a number of other branches, including: a Teachers, Educational Research, General Statistics and Information Technology branch divided into sections whose responsibilities are indicated by their titles and which include a section responsible for teachers' pay throughout the maintained and university sectors; a Pensions branch for the DES; a Teachers' Supply and Training branch which is divided into five different units responsible for teacher supply, teacher training, giving economic advice to the Department, operational research and financial management initiatives; an Information branch; a small Establishments and Organisation branch; and, finally, a Legal branch including medical advisers. The last two branches are loosely attached to some of the other branches.

Within this framework of branches, the policy formulation of the DES is a complex exercise. At the highest level there is a policy steering group which has the following terms of reference according to the 1979 review of the DES:

(a) to coordinate departmental analyses and reviews of programmes; and
(b) to present information and advice to ministers against the background of public expenditure.

Two of the Deputy Secretaries have a formally constituted policy group to support them with terms of reference 'to review developments and to consider future policy in relation to either adult/higher/further education or education at school'.

The DES came in for severe criticism in the mid-1970s from the Organisation for Economic Cooperation and Development (OECD) who made three major comments on its planning procedures. Firstly, that it was too secretive; secondly, that it reacted to existing trends rather than actively considering new patterns of development; and, thirdly, that it was too narrow in its view of education, ignoring the actions of other government departments and failing to consider the wider role of education in a modern society. In 1976 an expenditure committee of the House of Commons took 'policy-making in the DES' as its subject. It confirmed the OECD's reported view that both the teachers and LEAs were opposed to this. They saw the interface and planning between education and other social factors (such as equality, health and social security and employment) as their concern and not that of the DES. Sir William Pile, the Permanent Secretary from 1970 to 1976, is reported as giving evidence to both the OECD and the House of Commons Select Committee concerning DES intervention in the curriculum. He had already prepared the way for the DES to become more involved by strengthening Her Majesty's Inspectorate and it is mainly due to him that the Yellow Book, which led to Prime Minister Callaghan's Ruskin speech, was ready when Callaghan wanted such information. We can therefore reflect on the point made at the beginning of Chapter 2 about the time that is seen as the start of centralising power and know that these two reports, together with Sir William Pile's work, gave strength to a DES which had begun to revert to the regulatory role of the Board of Education and away from the powers given to the Secretary of State by virtue of the 1944 Act. We shall consider two examples of this later in the chapter, but first let us look at Her Majesty's Inspectorate of Schools.

HER MAJESTY'S INSPECTORATE OF SCHOOLS

The primary function of HMI is to report to the Secretary of State on the efficiency of the educational system. Ever since their creation in 1839, their function has been to inspect and report. The earliest legislation emphasised HMI's right of access, but gave no guidelines on the form inspection should take. Indeed it seemed to suggest that inspection was everything that an Inspector did when entering an educational establishment. Similarly, Section 77 of the 1944 Education Act required the Secretary of State to cause inspections to be made but defined neither the purpose nor the nature of such inspections.

In reporting on the efficiency of the educational system, HMI assess standards and trends throughout the system and on that basis report to the Permanent Secretary and to the Secretary of State on the state of the system nationally. The basis for all HMI's work is inspection which may take many forms ranging from short informal visits by one Inspector to one establishment through a full inspection of one establishment by a number of Inspectors, to a national survey conducted in several hundred establishments over a period of one or more years by several teams of Inspectors. A recent innovation amongst HMI is whole authority inspections of which, at the time of writing, several have been carried out.

Another function of HMI that was laid down in the letter of instruction to the first HMI in 1840, is to contribute towards improvements in the work they are called upon to inspect. In doing so they provide services to the Secretary of State's partners in the education system. These are services which, apart from their value to the partners, facilitate the work of inspection, and can range from a response to an individual teacher's question on a school visit to the provision of national short courses for teachers, to publications such as the *National Primary Survey*, or to the series of booklets on different curriculum areas produced in the mid-1980s. In this context HMI carries out a great deal of public speaking at national, regional or local level.

Within these functions the Inspectorate has a great deal of independence. Indeed, its very position is strange, and is one that almost defies definition. The DES itself describes the Inspectorate as 'working closely with the Department'. Yet the terms of reference to the Rayner scrutiny in December 1980 spoke of 'arrangements for collaboration between the Inspectorate and the rest of the DES . . .'. Whilst all the organisation charts on the DES show the Senior Chief Inspector as having line management to the Permanent Secretary, there is also unrestricted direct access to the Secretary of State. The Permanent Secretary is responsible to the Secretary of State for the whole of the Department and is accounting officer to Parliament for the expenditure of the Department as a whole, including the Inspectorate. Yet it is quite clear that in practice the Inspectorate is being allowed substantial freedom to develop and manage both its professional responses to the needs of ministers and the service it offers to those in LEAs, the voluntary bodies and the individual establishments that provide education. Moreover, whilst the right to decide whether to publish what HMI writes lies with the Secretary of State, there is a well accepted convention that anything that is published will be as HMI wrote it. Despite this apparent freedom for the Inspectorate, it is a highly structured and organised body, although individual Inspectors enjoy a marked degree of professional freedom.

ORGANISATION OF HER MAJESTY'S INSPECTORATE OF SCHOOLS

Before considering the present organisation of HMI, a very brief look at how they came into existence will be useful. We have already seen that the Inspectorate was established in 1839 and that the first reaction of the voluntary bodies, especially the Church of England, was hostile. In 1840 a concordat was reached which allowed the Archbishops of Canterbury and York to produce short lists from which Inspectors would be drawn. Shortly afterwards it proved necessary to make similar arrangements with the other denominations. This denominational arrangement lasted until 1870 and caused tremendous problems with seven different sets of Inspectors for England, Wales and Scotland, of which four sets – Church of England, Roman Catholic, British and Foreign, and Workhouse schools – covered the whole of England.

The 1870 Education Act led to a reorganisation of the Inspectorate and the concordat ceased as the inspection of religious education was removed from the fields of study falling within the competence of the Inspectorate. From 1870 onwards they were organised on a territorial basis with each Inspector responsible for the testing and inspection of all schools in a district. After

1902, with the testing aspect gone, there began a system which involved a full inspection of all schools every five years. This lasted until well after the 1944 Act though the cycle lengthened. Now full inspections are used on a very different basis. Between 1902 and 1944 there were several sets of Inspectors – elementary, secondary and technical. In 1944 they were merged into one Inspectorate and there were in that year 483 Inspectors. Since then there has been a doubling of the number of schoolchildren in the country, though the number has fallen back of late, yet the establishment for Inspectors in HMI is 430 in England and 60 in Wales. These Inspectors are organised in two ways: in a regional structure and in a national structure, with most Inspectors being placed in both structures. The exceptions to this are the Senior Chief Inspector, the Chief Inspectors and some other Inspectors who are based at the DES and who form the major link on matters of policy and planning between officers of the Department and the rest of the Inspectorate. All other members of HMI are assigned to one of the seven divisions of the country, each of which is under the general direction of a divisional Staff Inspector. A division will have between 40 and 65 Inspectors and, from these, at least two – one for schools and one for further/higher education – are nominated to each LEA as District Inspectors. This allows for easy communication both within the LEA and the territorial structure of the DES, especially in the schools branch. Other Inspectors obviously visit both schools and colleges within the LEAs in the division. Alongside the divisional structure is a mechanism for organising HMI on a national basis in terms of their phase, subject to aspect specialism as follows:

Phase

This refers to particular age groups such as nursery, primary, middle, secondary, 14–19 or further. There are national teams of phase specialists working under the general direction of the Staff Inspectors. The teams are distributed amongst the divisions and come together for planning purposes in both divisional and national committees chaired by Staff and Chief Inspectors.

Subject

There is a range of national subject teams under the direction of a Staff Inspector or an Inspectorate with national responsibility for a subject. These teams, both for schools and FE, come together in some thirty-five national subject committees.

Aspect

These are national responsibilities organised across phases and subjects. They include teams on special education and the inspection of independent schools. Some such teams are almost permanent while others are formed and disbanded as the need arises.

The management of HMI (like its place within the education system) is complex and all Inspectors have some responsibility for it. All have territorial responsibilities, all have phase responsibilities and some have subject responsibilities. All HMIs are responsible for and to a number of people. The hierarchy of HMI is a senior management team consisting of a Senior Chief Inspector and six Chief Inspectors, all of whom have responsibility for one or more aspects of the education system such as: primary and secondary education; special education; independent schools; European schools; service schools; careers education; further education; initial and in-service training of teachers; and external relations and publications. This team is concerned with overall priorities and the management of the inspection programme, staff development and the general development of the education service.

In 1981 the Rayner scrutiny made reference to various aspects of HMI and in 1983 a policy statement was published which recommended, amongst other things, that the level of formal reporting should be maintained at about 260 reports a year including reports on entire LEAs. It confirmed the previous announcement that all reports of formal inspections would be publicly available and that LEAs would have to respond to the reports, stating what action they intended to take on any recommendations. Here again is an example of the strengthening of central control.

Let us now turn to two areas of education and development and consider how the DES has influenced them since 1944. It will help us to understand the role of the DES in the educational system. The areas we shall look at are examinations and the curriculum.

The 1944 education Act scarcely mentions the curriculum. Indeed, excepting Religious Education it simply stated that, with the exception of Aided secondary schools, secular instruction should be under the control of an LEA unless otherwise provided for in the Articles of Government. The only other help given in the Act was that pupils should be educated according to their age, aptitude and ability. However, all this changed as a result of the 1988 Education Reform Act which introduced a National Curriculum for England and Wales. During the 1960s there were stirrings of dissatisfaction with the curriculum in schools and this, coupled with two adverse reports on the role of the DES (one in 1975 from the OECD and one the following year from the House of Commons Expenditure Committee), led the DES to begin to take a larger part in the determination of the curriculum which up to then had been teacher led. The main protagonist in this was the then Permanent Under-Secretary at the Department of Education and Science, Sir William Pile. Also in 1976 the then Prime Minister, Jim Callaghan, made a speech at Ruskin College, Oxford, regarding education and at the same time extracts were leaked from a DES 'Yellow Paper'. These events were followed by a series of regional conferences which became known in educational circles as the 'Great Debate'. In 1977 following on from this debate the DES published a Green Paper entitled 'Education in Schools – a consultative document' and followed it up with Circular 14/77 entitled 'LEA Arrangements for the School Curriculum'. This asked LEAs to consider the curriculum in all of their schools; it also led to a remark from one leading Chief Education Officer that 'it came as something of a shock to some LEAs to discover that they were held to a major curricular responsibility'.[2] The publication of the results of the survey in November 1979 (after the general election) is generally taken to mark a new stage in the move towards a central control of the curriculum. Following on from the survey the DES published a document entitled 'A Framework for the Curriculum' to which HMI responded with one entitled 'A View of the Curriculum'. Two years later, in 1981, a further document 'The School Curriculum' was published. HMI have also begun to publish a series of documents on the whole curriculum and on various aspects of it. In 1981 and 1983 the DES issued circulars to LEAs requiring them to take action on the curriculum. Again one leading Chief Education Officer commented that from 1977 to 1985 the 'HMI and DES between them published as much on curriculum as they published previously in the years since the 1870 Education Act.'[3] In March 1985 the White Paper 'Better Schools' made it clear that the Government wanted national agreement on the objectives and content of the school curriculum but national syllabuses were not contemplated. Yet two years later, after another electoral victory the Conservative Government entered upon hasty consultation before publishing the Education Reform Bill which was to become in largely unchanged form, the 1988 Education Reform Act and the biggest single piece of educational legislation since 1944. During the very short Consultation period in the summer and autumn of 1987 documents were issued calling not only for a natioanl curriculum and a national syllabus but also for the testing of children in certain subjects at the ages of 7, 11, 14 and 16.

All of this had been made possible by the abolition in 1984 of the Schools Council which had influenced the curriculum since its inception in 1964. The Schools Council was an organisation that was controlled dually by the LEAs and the Teachers Association. In practice, all curriculum matters were left to the Teachers' Association which, because of their dominance, was effectively the National Union of Teachers. However, one of the most vigorous supporters of the Schools Council was the Association of Education Committees (AEC) mainly through its Secretary, Sir William (later Lord) Alexander. It is significant that when the Schools Council met its untimely end in 1984 the AEC itself had been disbanded for some seven years. The authoritative voice on education administration in this period is of the opinion that 'the disappearance of the Schools Council and the assertion of control over the curriculum and examinations by the Secretary of State twenty years later would have hardly been conceivable if Education Committees had still possessed any effective national organization.'[4]

For twenty years, working parties of the Schools Council introduced innovative new curriculum ideas, but the trend in the 1980s meant that that body was abolished and was replaced by the Secondary Examinations Council and the Schools Curriculum Development Committee.

In 1987 during the drafting of the Bill the Secretary of State announced that these two councils in turn would be abolished. They were replaced under Section 14 of the 1988 Education Reform Act by two Curriculum Councils (one for England, one for Wales) and a Schools Examination and Assessment Council set up to advise the Secretary of State on matters relating to the curriculum and its assessment. All the members of these councils are nominated by the Secretary of State and to them he has to refer all proposed orders relating to subject requirements, attainment targets and programmes of study. Thus, under the 1988 Education Reform Act the control of the curriculum has finally come home to rest with the Secretary of State for Education and Science and, of course, his Permanent officials in the DES. The other area in which the DES has been involved, and the other way in which the curriculum is controlled, is by examinations and tests. For decades the curricula of the primary schools were hidebound by the various selection procedures used at around the age of $10\frac{1}{2}$ years (but always misnamed the 11+) which selected children for one or another type of secondary school. These tests put a strong emphasis on the teaching of English and Arithmetic, but since the adoption by most LEAs of a comprehensive system of secondary education the curriculum in most primary schools has broadened considerably.

In secondary schools the problems of examinations have a long chequered history. The GCE examinations at 'O' and 'A' level were introduced in 1951. The minimum age for 'O' level was 16, which was intended to limit the examination to certain types of pupil and school and thus keep other types of school free from the constraints that examinations would place upon their curriculum. (It must be remembered that the school-leaving age at this time was fifteen.) However, by 1953 many educationists and certainly one of the most powerful, William Alexander, were convinced that there was a need for a leaving examination for the average pupil. Yet it was to be twelve years before the Certificate of Secondary Education (CSE) became available for such pupils. It had five grades, the first of which was to be equivalent to the 'O' level pass grade. Within a year of the introduction of the CSE there was a call for the two examinations to be merged. In 1970 the governing council of the Schools Council voted for a single examination system at 16+ and also set up a programme to study the feasibility of such an examination. In 1975 a report was issued stating that a common system was feasible and proposing an examination system that took in many of the features of CSE such as teacher-developed examinations and assessment of coursework. However, the next year, as has been seen, was marked by Callaghan's Ruskin speech and the move away from teacher control in curriculum matters. Added to this was the fact that there were technical difficulties in conducting a single examination over a wide range of abilities. So by 1978, largely as a result of the *Waddell Report* the idea of differentiated papers came into being. This meant that whilst there would be a single system of examining, a range of papers would be set that could cater for the extremes of the ability range. The Waddell proposals were set out in a White Paper 'Secondary School Examinations; a single system at 16+'. Yet in the same year a NUT report made no reference to differentiation. The Cockcroft Report on Mathematics published in 1982 referred to it, and the GCSE examinations which were taken for the first time in the summer of 1988, whilst being a common examination system, actually had differentiated examination papers and/or questions in many subjects. This system means that some candidates are not eligible for higher grades because of the route they take and decisions on this are taken as early as fourteen years of age.

It would be remiss to end this section without reflecting on central government's role in all this. Not only have the DES been involved in all the discussions on examinations, which after all has always been the role of central government even if they have not always undertaken it, but other departments and their quangos have become involved. Thus, since 1974, the establishment

– under the umbrella of the Department of Employment of the Manpower Services Commission (several times renamed, but now the Training Agency) – has influenced both curriculum and examinations. Through the Technical and Vocational Education Initiative it has, since 1982, made large sums of money directly available to LEAs for their schools for these initaitives. This project set out to renew and revitalise both curriculum content and pedagogy, and whilst it seems to have failed in one of its objectives of doing so across the ability range, it appears to have succeeded with the average and below. Equally, the Training Agency has brought new life to non-school examining bodies such as the Royal Society of Arts, City and Guilds of London Institute and the Business/Technician Education Council, mainly through its sponsorship of schemes for unemployed young people which includes a largely FE college-based training element which is examinable, if not in conventional ways.

The real boost for testing though, as we saw earlier, will be the examination or assessment of the vast majority of the nation's children on four occasions in their school career at the ages of 7, 11, 14 and 16. To assist in this matter the Secretary of State set up in mid-1987 a Task Group on Assessment and Testing (TGAT). This reported within five months and became the basis of a DES policy guide for the National Curriculum subject working groups set up to consider attainment targets, programmes of study and assessment arrangements. Thus we see that the control of the curriculum is strengthened through the control of examinations and assessment and that both these matters have now, as a result of the 1988 legislation, returned safely to the corridors of power in Whitehall.

REFERENCES

1. DES, 1985 *The DES – A Brief Guide*, HMSO
2. Fiske, D, 1979 *Journal of National Association of Inspectors and Educational Advisers*.
3. Brighouse, T, 1986 *Education*, **165**, p. 128.
4. G. Cooke and P. Gosden, 1986 *Education Committees* Councils and Educational Press, p. 67

FURTHER READING

As for Chapter 2 plus:
DES 1983 *Study of HMI in England and Wales*, HMSO.

Lawton, D. and Gordon, P. 1987 *HMI*, Routledge and Kegan Paul.
Pile, W. 1979 *The Department of Education and Science*, Allen and Unwin.
Salter, B and Tapper, T. 1981 *Education, Politics and the State*, Grant McIntyre.

The role of Local Education Authorities

As was discussed in the first chapter, there have been local education authorities (LEAs) in one form or another since 1870. Their role has changed tremendously since 1974 and seems destined to change even more since the passing of the 1988 Education Reform Act. What are these LEAs? In England and Wales they are legally the full councils of the 47 county councils, the 36 metropolitan districts, the 33 London boroughs and the Isles of Scilly. (Until 31 March 1990 the Inner London boroughs formed the Inner London Education Authority.) The authorities have different functions depending on whether they are a county or metropolitan/London District. One of the functions that they share is that they all have Social Services Departments. The local authorities in their present form (outside London) were established by the Local Government Act 1972 and within London by the Local Government Act 1963 together with the extra functions that they were given by the Education Reform Act 1988. At present there are 117 LEAs. They differ tremendously in size from a population of 1.5 million in Hampshire to 133,000 in Kingston-upon-Thames* and the number of councillors who make up the council differs accordingly. The county council elections are held every four years when all the members are returned. In the metropolitan districts and in the London boroughs a third of the members retire every year except in the year of county council elections when there are no elections in the districts or boroughs.

All the councillors elected form the council which meets on a regular basis, probably monthly or six-weekly, though in some large county councils there are still quarterly meetings. While the council may delegate its business to committees, sub-committees or even officers it is in full council itself that all major policy decisions are taken. Increasingly since the mid-1960s but especially since 1974 (the year in which the 1972 reforms were implemented) local government has become more political in its activities. Thus the major political parties on a council will hold caucus meetings and it is at these meetings that the party line on

---

* These figures do not include the tiny populations of the Isles of Scilly and the City of London.

a particular issue will be decided. This caucus may well be influenced by the national view of the party on certain issues, especially ones of national import, and it will almost certainly be influenced by the views of members of the party locally who are not councillors but who play a large part in local political affairs. Indeed, in most authorities where one party of whatever political persuasion has an overall majority, decisions will be made in party caucus meetings and though the debate may range long and hard in the council chamber the outcome of the debate is known in advance and never in doubt. The council may have a number of committees. Some, including the Education Committee are required by statute under Section 101(9) of the Local Government Act 1972. However, the most important committee of the council is the one that concerns itself with the allocation of resources and will be called by a title such as Policy and Resources Committee. The present committee structures of most councils owes a great deal to the ideas for the reform of the internal organisation of councils put forward by the Maud Committee on the Management of Local Government in 1967. This was then modified by the Baines Committee Report in 1972, which led to the adoption by many local authorities of a system of corporate management.

Whilst the Policy and Resources Committee will do exactly as it wants, before decisions can be implemented they must be passed by both the Education Committee and the full council. The case of Regina versus Kirklees *ex parte* Molley enforced this, including ensuring that in the case of decisions reached by Education Committees and confirmed by full council all members of the council had received copies of the appropriate documentation and the decisions were not simply 'nodded' through the full council.

Whilst an Education Committee is a statutory requirement, the way in which it operates and its composition may differ greatly. A traditional pattern is for an Education Committee to have a number of sub-committees where items are dealt with fully and then passed up to the Education Committee for confirmation. In some cases matters may be delegated to sub-committees and officers allowed to implement the decisions from the sub-committee rather than wait for approval by the full committee and/or council, although the minutes of the sub-committee will always be taken to both the full committee and the council meeting. The sub-committees have traditionally been for phases of the service or for broad aspects for example, school sub-committee; FE (or 16+) sub-committee; sites and buildings sub-committee; careers service sub-committee and finance sub-committee.

The work of the sub-committees will differ, depending on the composition of the council. Councils on which one political party has a large majority will be able to delegate decisions to sub-committees, safe in the knowledge that, apart from exceptional and unforeseen circumstances, the whips will ensure that the decisions are confirmed at the full committee or at council. Councils where there is a slender or no political control cannot act in this way, as the absence of just one member of a sub-committee can result in a decision that will then be changed at a later stage. This is more so in an Education Committee than in any other committee of the council because of the composition of the Education Committee. Whilst the majority of committees of a council are made up wholly of members of the council (although this is altering all the time) this is not so for the Education Committee, and has not been so since the 1902 Education Act. That Act, and all subsequent legislation, has required the Education Committee to include 'co-opted' members. There had been co-option to the Technical Instruction Committees which had been in existence since 1889. The 1902 Act widened the basis of membership of the Education Committee which was basically to 'appoint persons experienced in education and persons acquainted with the needs of various types of school within its (the LEA) area.' This could be done by selecting councillors with the right experience or co-opting people onto the Education Committee. The majority of Education Committees decided to co-opt and this process was again followed in 1944 and 1974. A schedule to the 1944 Act suggested that authorities might include amongst their co-optees representatives of the teaching profession, of religious interests, and of industry, commerce and agriculture. Before 1974 many LEAs co-opted after consultation especially with teachers' associations. Since then, particularly for teachers, there have emerged democratic ways of electing representatives to the Education Committee, usually one for each of the three phases of primary, secondary and further. Increasingly since 1974 co-options to Education Committees have been made from supporters of political parties. In many LEAs the combined strength of minority party councillors plus co-opted members has meant that they could outvote the majority party, who then had to have decisions reversed at full council. To counter this many schemes of co-option include people who are willing to follow a party whip with the majority party having enough co-options to ensure that it can win votes at all stages from sub-committees upwards. On any committee – and Education Committees despite their constitution are no exception – the effectiveness of the committee often depends on its leadership, and on the political side this leadership will be that of the Chair Person and Vice-Chair Person (we shall consider the role of officers later in this chapter). The Chair Person will not only be a member of the ruling party but is also likely to be an important member of that group. It will be the role of the Chair Person to negotiate education policy in the inner sanctums of the policy-making machinery of the ruling party, and then to see that that policy is carried out. The Chair Person, through close contact with officers, will become very knowledgeable on educational matters and if national office is also obtained then the educational knowledge, at least in political terms, will be second to none. During the 1980s such diverse figures as Josie Farrington of Lancashire, Philip Merridale of Hampshire, John Pearman of Wakefield and Neil Fletcher of ILEA. fulfiled such roles.

There is also the possibility that on certain councils the leader of the council will be a totally dominant figure and will require the Chair Person of the Education Committee to follow the leadership's commands. In this case the role will not be one of negotiation but simply one of ensuring that policy is carried out. A much more difficult role is that of the Chair Person of the Education Committee of a hung council. Here the problems outlined earlier come into play when it may be necessary to negotiate trade-offs with groups of members both elected and co-opted to ensure political success. There are real political problems if a decision taken at one level is overturned at another. The public will have been informed through the media of the first decision and may well turn against the political party that rescinds what may have been a popular decision. It is probably easiest to illustrate this by example. The majority party on a council reacted to Circular 2/82 on School Places by putting forward a list of schools it wished to consider for closure. Prior to issuing Section 12 Notices, consultation meetings had taken place and a report was put before the Education Committee. The report included a full account of the feelings of the public – parents, teachers and governors, etc. – at the consultation meeting. The recommendation of the officers was that despite objections (there nearly always are objections to closures) the whole plan should go ahead. The minority parties plus the co-opted members successfully voted for an amendment to keep one school open. This was reported in the press and the strong action group in the community involved was jubilant. The school happened to be within a ward that was very marginal and was held by the ruling group. Despite this, at a pre-council meeting the ruling group confirmed their decision that they wanted to issue Section 12 Notices to close *all* the schools on the list. There was criticism of the Chair Person of Education for allowing one school to get away, especially as a reversal of the decision at full council would make the group unpopular with the community and might lose them a seat at the next election. Nevertheless, the prevailing view amongst councillors was that if one particular school was not put forward as a candidate for closure, why should a school in their ward be put forward? The result was that all the schools were put forward for closure. Almost a non-win situation for a Chair Person who, after all, can only count on the support of his or her own party. Because of this there has been some questioning of the principles of co-option and a court ruling Regina versus Croydon London Borough Council *ex parte* Leney suggests that there is no need for co-options if in fact the requirement of the 1944 Act can be met from within the Education Committee. This begins to suggest that there may well be alterations to the composition of Education Committees in the future.

The Widdicombe Enquiry into the conduct of local authority business, which reported in 1986, recommended that 'decision-making committees and sub-committees may only consist of Councillors, and in particular only councillors may vote on such committees.' This recommendation was made about co-options in general. In fact the committee were unable to make a decision on the question of education co-option, and recommended that this view be reviewed by the Government. The committee was not happy about the current arrangements on Education Committees however, questioning why teachers should be able to demand 'a right' co-option when, for example, parents could not claim such a right. A recent White Paper has suggested that legislation will shortly be put before Parliament to take away co-options from Education Committees and that in fact the present co-opted member will simply be there in an advisory capacity.

EDUCATION OFFICERS

As we have already seen, some LEAs can trace their origins back to the School Boards and perhaps the most famous of them was the former ILEA which, until its demise in 1990, was coterminous with the area of the original London School Board. The LEAs that are able to do this are those in cities and urban areas where the School Board would often cover the area of the county borough. In the Shire counties, 1902 meant the takeover of a number of School Boards. Education Offices often reflect their heritage and there will be different practices in them. It is likely that in some authorities, especially the county ones, they will be responsible for the library service, although this is also true of some metropolitan districts. Other authorities may give the control of their youth services and education welfare services to other committees. Since 1974, with the growth of corporate management, many of the functions which education departments carried out for themselves are now undertaken centrally, thus the few education departments which still had architects departments have lost them to central architects departments; the clerking of committees has been transferred to the County Secretary or the clerks department, while some financial functions have been transferred to the Treasurers and will increasingly do so as schools have delegated financial management under the terms of the 1988 Education Reform Act. Indeed this Act is increasingly likely to alter the whole role of the Education Officer. Many of the functions which were carried out centrally in the past will be carried out within the school. It may well be that many LEAs will simply become centres for quality control relying heavily on their advisory and inspectorial role to ensure that the schools which have delegated power are keeping within the remit of the 1988 Education Reform Act on that delegated power and also carrying out the requirements of that Act for the National Curriculum and Assessment. The most important function which has left education departments is that of personnel. With the delegation to schools of much responsibility for appointing their own staff, there may still be a central payroll function, but the only personnel role left to the Education Officer is the right to be present and advise on the appointment of Heads and Deputies and to be invited to take part in other teaching appointments. In most authorities the personnel functions of all non-teaching staff already lies in the Personnel Department but this increasingly will be delegated to the schools as they receive their own budgets.

The basic work of all education departments is very similar, but obviously the size of education departments differs considerably and this reflects on the number and workload of officers. Prior to local government reorganisation in 1974, Her Majesty's Inspectorate recommended a minimum population for an LEA of 400,000; the Royal Commission, one of 250,000. Yet in 1974 there were seventeen authorities that had populations of less than that and the demise of ILEA in 1990 will add twelve more to that number. Only Wandsworth of the Inner London boroughs has a population of more than 250,000. Many of the larger county LEAs organise their departments on an area basis, having an office in County Hall and area offices scattered around the county. These area offices often carry out tasks that senior officers in a central office do in other authorities.

Most education departments are organised on a hierarchical basis and Figure 4.1 shows a typical structure. From that figure can be seen the wide range of professional posts in an education department. As well as the pure administrators there are advisers, careers officers, psychologists, welfare officers and school meals organisers. Each of these disciplines will be organised and managed on a hierarchial bases. We shall look at the structure of the office shown in the figure and consider what each discipline does and how the officers have reached their positions. In considering this matter we must realise that as this book goes to press the whole concept of the work of a local education officer is altering.

The chief education officer

Whilst this is the legal title of the person who heads the Education Department, the title Director of Education is also used and in Cornwall the title Secretary is still used. This person will almost certainly be an ex-graduate teacher who taught for a period and then entered an education office either as a Professional (or Administrative) Assistant or as an Assistant Education Officer. There are notable exceptions to this and one or two appointments recently have been made from principals or head teachers of education institutions who have little or no experience of administration in a local education office. This, perhaps, reflects the changing role in relationships between school and education office and is a result of the 1988 legislation. In the normal course of events, after possibly three or four years in the first post, there will be a move to a more senior post followed by a move to a Deputy Chief Education Officer followed by promotion (quite often within the same authority) to become Chief Education Officer. The Chief Education Officer is responsible to the committee for the work of the whole office and of the education service within the authority. He or she may also be part of the Authority's corporate management structure.

Deputy chief education officer

The tier below the Chief Education Officer (CEO) is the one at which there is really no common pattern. Whilst, as we have seen, the most senior post is a statutory one, there is a great debate concerning the next tier of responsibility. The Baines Report, published shortly before local government reorganisation in 1972, recommended the abolition of the post of Deputy Chief Officer in all departments, yet most local authorities ignored the suggestion. We are therefore left with a number of situations: in some authorities there is one deputy, in others two or even three with one of them being specifically named as the 'first' deputy, i.e. the person who substitutes for the CEO in that person's absence. In other authorities there is no deputy, but one of the post-holders of the next tier down will usually be designated to act as the CEO when necessary.

Whilst there are strong arguments against a deputy, there are stronger ones for it. The major points in favour of a deputy are that at least one of the persons needs to be able to take an overall view of the service, that there is a need for one person to assume

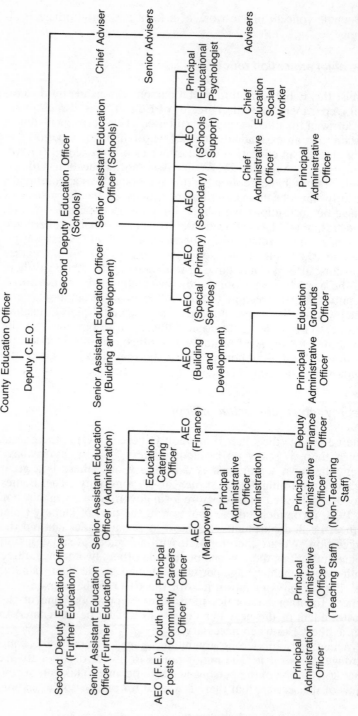

Fig. 4.1 Education Department – Central Administration structure

responsibility in the CEO's absence, and it is useful to have someone other than the CEO who can coordinate the rest of the management team within the office.

Quite often a deputy will have these responsibilities and also responsibility for specific or perhaps one-off problems which do not fall neatly into any of the various branches into which an education office is divided.

Third tier officers

Let us now turn to these branches. In our diagram (Figure 4.1) there are five people at what is shown as third tier level (but could equally be second tier in some organisational charts). We shall not look at the post of Chief Inspector/Adviser at present but shall return to that post later because it is not a post which heads a branch of the office in the operational way. There are therefore the four posts of SAEO for Schools, Further Education, Administration, and Building and Development. These posts will differ from office to office both in their nomenclature and in responsibilities. Thus, in some offices the FE posts may well be named 16+, while in some smaller offices the latter two posts may well be held by one person. These post-holders tend to carry out the tasks that the name suggests, though of course this is far too simplistic a statement. Thus, whilst the schools post will be responsible for most of the things that concern the school in a LEA there will be matters over which control is held elsewhere. Thus the Buildings and Development person will be responsible for the administrative tasks concerned with planning new schools, closing existing ones, and actually making sure that schools are built, extended and repaired. Equally that person will be responsible in the same way for all other educational buildings. So whilst the head of the Schools branch has managerial responsibility for that branch, there is also the need for sideways involvement with other branches. This, of course, does not only apply at this level but all the way down through the hierarchy. To return to the Schools branch, it can be seen by referring to Fig. 4.1 the post holder is responsible for such matters as staffing, school adminstration, governing bodies and special services. While a great deal of this work has be delegated to schools as a result of both the 1986 (No 2) and 1988 Education Acts there is still a great deal to be done in the education office. The same can be said for the SAEO (FE) or (16+.) Whilst the 1988 Act has removed virtually all higher education from the LEAs and has also given much greater power to the governors of the other colleges, there is still a great deal to do in the education office in making sure that the general post-16 policy of the authority is carried out. This person, as well as having the oversight of the FE colleges, will also be concerned with the work of the youth and community service (except in those very few LEAs where this is the responsibility of a department other than education). He/she will also be involved in the regional organisation of further education and will quite often represent the CEO at meetings of the Regional Advisory Council for Further and Higher Education. Again, as with the SAEO (Schools), if this officer's responsibility is for 16+ then he/she will have to liaise with schools and colleges especially when institutions which cross the 16+ divide are concerned.

We saw earlier that the third officer at this level has control of Buildings and Development. In the 1950s–70s this would often have been the most complex and often the most exciting job in the office, as the LEAs built massively to provide schools for the increasing child population, but also to fulfill the aims of the 1944 Education Act of secondary education for all. Today, with falling or stable school rolls, this post is one of retrenchment, of rationalising school places, and perhaps only building a new school when this allows two or three others to be closed. The officer who holds this post will also be responsible for the fabric of the buildings themselves and this is an area where, with restrictions on local government expenditure, real savings have had to be made. Consequently HMI has reported pessimistically on the state of school buildings, and the maintenance of fabric is a major problem for governing bodies under the new schemes of financial delegation. It is likely that in fact some maintenance items may well be kept within an education office. Because of the financial delegation to schools resulting from the 1988 Act, the task of the final officer at this level has changed considerably. Increasingly the finance department of a local authority has been brought in to work out the scheme of financial delegation, but until 1994 this officer will be responsible for making sure that the transition from a centrally controlled budget to a schools controlled budget goes smoothly. It will also be the responsibility of this officer to ensure that schools that are not part of a financial delegation scheme also operate within the rules of such schemes. This officer will also have to ensure that schools that do have delegated powers are operated correctly and he/she will make reports on situations where governing bodies need to have their power of delegation withdrawn.

Advisers/inspectors

The majority of authorities will have a team of Inspectors again organised on a hierarchical structure. This will be headed by a

Chief Adviser/Inspector who will often have senior Inspectors/Advisers for the various phases together with Advisers often on a subject or in the case of primary on an age basis. Because of the legislation on the National Curriculum and on Attainment and Testing the team of Advisers within local authorities is to be increased. It is the responsibility of the LEAs to ensure, along with the governors of both county and voluntary schools, that the National Curriculum is taught in the schools and that testing is carried out at the relevant ages. In the light of this, the role of the Advisory Service is likely to alter considerably. Already some LEAs are beginning to think seriously about the complementary role of Advisers/Administrators and to restructure their offices to ensure that both types of officer go out into schools and carry out increasingly different roles of the LEA as a result of the 1988 education legislation. For many Advisers this brings about an inspectorial role of the type that they have not previously come across. Many Advisers in the past have simply been propounders of good practice; in the future they will have to return much more to the inspectorial role from whence the Advisory Service came in the early years of this century.

It is likely that over the next decade the role of the LEA and the education office will change beyond recognition from that which it played between 1944 and 1988. There are many leaders of the education service who can actually foresee the demise of the LEA and a pre-1902 position returned to; that of a direct relationship between a central government department (perhaps aided by regional education authorities) and the schools. It may not be long after this book is published before we know whether this is likely to happen.

FURTHER READING

Brooksbank, K. and Ackstine, A. 1989 *Educational Administration*, Councils and Educational Press.

Bush, T. and Kogan, M. 1982 *Directors of Education*, Allen and Unwin.

Cooke, G. and Gosden, P. 1986 *Education Committees*, Councils and Educational Press.

DES 1983 Study of HMI *in England and Wales*, HMSO.

DES 1985 *The DES – A Brief Guide*, HMSO.

Fenwick, I. and McBride, P. 1982 *The Government of Education in Britain*, Martin Robertson.

Gosdon, P. H. J. H. 1983 T*he Educational System since 1944*, Martin Robertson.

Lawton, D. and Gordon, P. 1987 *HMI*. Routledge and Kegan Paul.

MacClure, S. 1988 *Education Reformed*, Hodder and Stoughton.

Pile, W. 1979 *The Department of Education and Science*, Allen and Unwin.

Ranson, S. and Tomlinson, J. (eds) 1986 *The Changing Government of Education*, Allen and Unwin.
Regan, D. 1984 *Local Government and Education*, Allen and Unwin.
Salter, B. and Tapper, T. 1981 *Education, Politics and the State*, Grant McIntyre.
Winckley, C. 1985 *Diplomats and Detectives*, Robert Royce.

CHAPTER 5

How the money is spent and how the bills are paid

Teachers and students often respond negatively and uninterestedly when issues of the finance of education are raised – indeed, groans and yawns have been known to echo around staff rooms and lecture halls. Educational finance is frequently seen as technical and complex and devoid of human interest. Although teachers and students are right to regard finance as a topic which requires concentration and careful study, they should not be put off by this. Questions of resources and cash have powerful influences over the nature and quality of contemporary educational provisions and they are neglected by teachers and students at their peril. From young pre-school children to ministers and senior civil servants at the DES, money impinges on the educational lives of us all. We may wish to see finance as a second-order issue in education, but in countries such as England and Wales with their long-term economic problems, it is hardly possible to consider questions of teaching and learning without continual reference to costs. Finance often appears to involve less human interaction than most other aspects of the educational process, but this is a superficial impression. The struggle to control 'the purse strings' is about power, and this is no less true of the education service than other aspects of life. The conventions and practices of educational finance usually seem and sometimes are complex, technical and beyond the scope of all except a few initiated senior administrators, but this does not imply that they are 'neutral'. Despite outward appearances, material interests of various kinds are being pursued and often vigorous human interactions are taking place. The results of these interactions soon deeply affect the daily lives of pupils and teachers working in classrooms.

Educational expenditure expanded steadily in the 1950s and then more rapidly in the 1960s and the very early 1970s. This growth was not merely a reflection of inflation. Expenditure on the education service grew substantially in real terms. Expressed simply this means that, when due allowance is made for the changing value of money, there were important increases in the financial resources devoted to education. During this period the numbers of pupils in schools and students in higher education increased in line with the demographic trends in society. Policies such as raising the school-leaving age, extending the length of teacher training courses and widening opportunities for young people in higher education, also augmented the number of customers for the education service. Those who worked in education during these years often began to regard growth as 'normal, natural and inevitable'. In the late 1960s Sir William Alexander, Secretary to the Association of Education Committees, saw that expansion could not go on for ever and he regularly warned his colleagues in the service of more difficult times ahead.

By the early 1970s ominous trends in the birth-rate were visible and by the mid-1970s primary school rolls began to fall. Teacher shortage became teacher surplus. Colleges of education were the first institutions to witness redundancies in the service. Around the same time the oil crisis of 1973 forced politicians of all parties to reconsider their programme for public expenditure. During the mid-1970s economic growth in this country was very limited, and consequently for some years public expenditure continued to grow faster than the economy as a whole. Although educationists felt increasingly threatened, the service still remained relatively cushioned from the full force of the changed economic and financial circumstances. It was the election in 1979 of a Conservative Government committed to reducing the proportion of national resources devoted to the public services that transformed the situation. From the outset the Conservatives made it clear that education, particularly with prevailing demographic trends and falling rolls, would have to take its full share of cuts in public expenditure. Education was not to be offered the kind of protection given to areas such as defence and law and order enforcement. At the same time the Government's economic policy of 'squeezing inflation out of the system' contributed considerably to further increases in unemployment. This, in turn, led to a need for more public expenditure on benefits. In addition, this country's ageing population, with people retiring earlier and living longer, has necessarily put up expenditure on pensions and health care. In the 1980s, therefore, education has had to compete against other services with important and growing needs for funds in a political setting inimical to public expenditure generally. There can be little doubt that the education service in the 1980s has operated in the most adverse financial climate since the war. Many, although not all, would argue that the quality of the service provided has suffered as a result of the real reductions in expenditure that have been made. At its peak in 1975–76 education spending accounted for 6.3 per cent of Gross Domestic Product. During the first half of the 1980s this percentage was never above 5.5 and in 1985–86 it was down to 4.8[1] – a significant fall from the position a decade earlier. In the budget for the financial year 1987–88 it was proposed that

10 per cent of public expenditure should be devoted to education and science.[2] This put education in fourth place (behind social security taking 27 per cent, defence 11 per cent and health and personal social services 11 per cent) amongst the major services involving expenditure of public funds. These relative positions were held during the late 1980s.

It is now opportune to consider how educational expenditure is divided between the different sectors of the service.[3] Table 5.1 summarises the essential information conveniently.

TABLE 5.1
Total Net Expenditure by sector of education, 1985–86

	Percentage of total education budget
Secondary schools	28.9
Primary schools	21.0
Universities	9.8
Non-advanced further education	7.0
Student awards	6.1
Advanced further education	5.6
Central administration and research	5.4
Other schools	3.7
School transport	3.1
School meals and milk	3.1
Youth service	0.9
Adult education	0.8
Nursery education	0.3
Total capital expenditure	4.3

There have been few major changes in the proportions taken by the different sectors set out in Table 5.1 during the 1980s. Schools regularly account for rather more than half of the expenditure and post-school education (excluding student awards) for approaching a quarter. There is some evidence, however, that the Government wished to devote less money to some of the ancillary services provided. Soon after the Conservatives came into office it was announced that economies were expected in education and the then Secretary of State indicated that 80 per cent of the required economies could be achieved from savings in the areas of school meals, milk and transport.[4] The Government gave these services low priority and encouraged those in local government to do the same. The House of Lords, however, prevented the cuts in school transport and many LEAs continued to provide school meals services and milk for children in primary schools at levels regarded as generous by the Government. In consequence, despite Government intentions, school meals, milk and transport often remained important items in LEA budgets and, thus, larger reductions had to be made in schools' direct educational expenditure on, for example, books, stationery and equipment.

TABLE 5.2
**Local authority gross recurrent educational expenditure by category:
1985–86**

	%
Teachers' and lecturers' salaries	52.2
Premises	10.1
Non-teaching staff	9.1
Fees, awards and allowances	7.6
School meals and milk	5.1
Education support staff	4.1
Other education expenditure	3.2
Establishment expenses	3.1
Equipment	2.6
Transport	2.2
Books	0.7

Table 5.2 shows how educational expenditure can be divided into constituent categories.[5] Taking teaching and non-teaching staff together, almost two-thirds of the available funds in 1985–86 were spent on salaries. In earlier periods an even greater proportion of expenditure was devoted to remunerating staff, and it is likely that in the 1980s education is more capital intensive than it has ever been before. Nonetheless, education remains a classic example of a labour-intensive industry, and this can have important consequences for the service if wages in the economy as a whole rise faster than the prices of other commodities. Teachers and others employed in education will, understandably, expect their remuneration and living standards to keep pace with general trends in society, yet, if they succeed in achieving their expectations, because education is more labour intensive than many other industries, the relative cost of providing the education service will go up disproportionately.

Throughout the 1980s teachers' pay and conditions of service have been controversial issues given wide coverage in the media. Inevitably television and the newspapers have chosen to give attention to the more spectacular aspects of industrial action and to confrontation. Comparatively few attempts have been made, at least in the popular media, to analyse in a dispassionate manner why and how the nation's schools and colleges have experienced such troubled times in the recent past.

From 1919 to 1987 the Burnham Committee dealt with the question of national pay scales for teachers, but it had no jurisdiction over conditions of service issues. Burnham was a large committee involving about sixty members with an independent chairman appointed by government. Members were divided into opposing panels, one representing management and the other the teachers. Until 1965 local authority association representatives

formed the whole of the management panel, but at that time two
DES representatives were added with weighted voting rights
which gave them greater influence than their numerical strength
suggested. It was also agreed between the then Government and
the local authorities that no claim could be accepted or offer
made if the Secretary of State objected to the total cost
involved.[6] Membership of the teachers' panel varied from time
to time, but in the mid-1980s the teachers' associations were
represented in the following proportions: National Union of
Teachers 13, Secondary Heads Association 1, Assistant Masters
and Mistresses Association 4, National Association of Head
Teachers 2, National Association of Schoolmasters/Union of
Women Teachers 7, Professional Association of Teachers 1. The
management and teachers' panels met separately, and in full
committee it was conventional for each side to speak 'with a
single voice'. Over the years the Burnham Committee became
ritualistic with the leaders of the two panels, with occasional
contributions from the Chairman, totally dominating the
proceedings. Negotiations did not take place around the table in
any meaningful sense, and both sides became increasingly frus-
trated. Both the local authorities and the teachers knew that it
would be the Government, and not the negotiators, which took
the ultimate important decisions. By the early 1980s there was
consensus that the Burnham machinery did not work well but
there was little hope of agreement about what should replace it.
The Government wanted to consider the questions of pay and
conditions together, but this was resisted by the unions. Teachers
believed that their pay, like that of some other groups of workers
in the public services, was falling considerably behind the remuneration of comparable employees in the private sector. They
also held that cuts in public expenditure were doing irreparable
damage to the service in which they worked and that children's
interests and life chances were suffering. By 1985 many teachers
felt that this situation could be tolerated no longer and they
became involved in a protracted and bitter industrial dispute
which included strikes and other forms of action.

It would be wrong to imply that this dispute was settled
amicably. It was eventually brought to an end when the Secretary
of State imposed the Teachers' Pay and Conditions Act, 1987.
This abolished the Burnham Committee and took away the
teachers' and the local authorities' negotiating rights. This
incensed the teachers who fought these proposals bitterly, but the
Government was in no mood to adopt a more conciliatory
position. In this new legislation questions of teachers' pay and
conditions of service were closely linked, thus achieving one of
the Government's primary objectives. To replace Burnham, an
Interim Advisory Committee has been appointed by the Govern-

ment to examine and report on matters relating to teachers' pay and conditions referred to it by the Secretary of State. After receiving advice from this committee, the Secretary of State is expected to consult the local authority associations, bodies representing the governors of voluntary schools and the teachers' unions before he takes steps to implement the recommendations of the committee, with or without modification. Clearly the local authorities and the teachers' unions are now in a much weaker position than they were under Burnham. It is envisaged that this machinery will operate until the end of March 1990, and, after then, the Government has proposed the establishment of a Teachers' Negotiating Group. If these ideas are implemented, the Secretary of State's representatives will have a majority of the votes on the management side. If the Group fails to reach agreement there will be the possibility of arbitration, but there will also 'be provision, for the management side to break the deadlock by implementing its proposals subject to the approval of Parliament'.[7]

The structure of teachers' salary scales was also changed radically in 1987 as a result of legislation and subsequent orders. A new departure in the Act gave the Secretary of State the power to introduce, with Parliament's agreement, different salary provisions for different cases. This means that, without recourse to further legislation, teachers' remuneration can be varied between, for example, different parts of the country, different types of schools and different subjects taught. As yet the Secretary of State has not used this power, and in October 1987 one main scale on which all teachers except heads and deputies are paid was introduced.[8] Table 5.3 sets out this main scale.

TABLE 5.3
Main scale paid from April 1989

Scale point	Annual Salary £
1	8,394
2	8,730
3	9,060
4	9,390
5	10,167
6	11,046
7	11,712
8	12,372
9	13,092
10	13,923
11	14,694

Graduates entering teaching are normally appointed to scale point 2 and 'good' honours graduates to point 4.

Five levels of incentive allowances (from allowance A worth £858 per annum to allowance E worth £4,710 per annum at 1988–90 rates) are available for some experienced teachers. Incentive allowances can now be held by teachers who fall into at least one of the following categories: (1) those who undertake responsibilities beyond those common to the majority of teachers; (2) those who demonstrate outstanding abilities as classroom teachers; (3) those employed to teach shortage subjects; (4) those employed in posts difficult to fill. The number and level of incentive allowances available in any particular school are controlled by its 'unit total', sometimes called colloquially its 'points score'. A school's unit total is determined largely by the number of pupils on roll and their ages (for example, each pupil under 14 normally counts as 2 units and each pupil over 17 counts as 9 units). Unit totals also control the group sizes allocated to schools, and these in turn determine the salaries received by their heads and deputies. Table 5.4 illustrates how this works.

TABLE 5.4
Unit total, school groups, and salaries of heads and deputies

Unit total	School group	Head's annual salary 1989–90 £	Deputy's annual salary 1989–90 £
Up to 100	1	17,370	16,527
101 to 200	2	17,928	16,527
201 to 300	3	18,489	16,527
301 to 500	4	19,050	16,809
501 to 700	5	19,893	17,229
701 to 1000	6	21,288	17,646
1,001 to 1,300	7	22,410	18,207
1,301 to 1,800	8	23,811	19,050
1,801 to 2,400	9	25,491	20,169
2,401 to 3,300	10	27,171	21,288
3,301 to 4,600	11	29,136	22,131
4,601 to 6,000	12	31,095	23,253
6,001 to 7,600	13	32,496	24,093
Over 7,600	14	34,179	24,933

In addition to salaries, the Act of 1987 also dealt with teachers' conditions of service. For some years governments, and particularly the Conservative administrations elected since 1979, had been dissatisfied with a situation in which teachers' pay and conditions were negotiated separately. As has been indicated, the Burnham machinery controlled salaries, but, from 1974, a working group known as the Council of Local Education Authorities/School Teachers (CLEA/ST) regulated teachers' conditions. The Government was not involved with this group which was made up of representatives of the local authority associations and the teachers' unions. Agreements made in CLEA/ST were codified in a document often referred to as 'the burgundy book'. It covered matters such as grievances and disciplinary procedures, leave of absence and travelling allowances. It did not define teachers' duties or their working time. During the industrial dispute of the mid-1980s, there were two issues in the conditions of service area which particularly annoyed the Government. Teachers maintained that dinner-time duties and the provision of cover for absent colleagues were matters of 'good will' and, therefore, voluntary. As part of the dispute many teachers withdrew their good will and refused to be involved with such activities. Consequently, in many schools children were dismissed from school premises at dinner times, and in some schools children were, from time to time, sent home because of staff absences. It must be stressed that teachers did not resort to such sanctions lightly, and they were only used because the teachers believed that a complete impasse had been reached in the industrial dispute. There can be little doubt, however, that the Government, as a result of this action, became more determined than ever to link questions of pay with conditions of service, and, furthermore, to take more central control. On the question of dinner-time duties, the Government eventually conceded and earmarked certain funds to pay midday supervisors. A teacher now has an unequivocal right to a break of a reasonable length at dinner time unless he or she chooses to be 'employed under a separate contract as a midday supervisor'.[9]

The Act of 1987 and subsequent orders have laid down teachers' conditions of service in a way that has never been previously attempted. Professional duties and working time have now been prescribed in great detail. Teachers' duties are subdivided into twelve categories and include all the following activities[10]

(1) teaching, including course- and lesson-planning, marking assessing and record-keeping;
(2) pastoral work with classes and individual pupils including communicating with parents and outside agencies and attending any meetings organised for these purposes;
(3) providing assessments and reports;
(4) participating in arrangements for teacher appraisal;
(5) reviewing teaching methods and programmes of work, participating in arrangements for further training and professional development;
(6) cooperating with the head teacher (or other teachers) in the development of courses, teaching materials, programmes, arrangements, etc.

(7) maintaining good order amongst pupils and safeguarding their health and safety;
(8) participating in staff meetings;
(9) covering for absent teachers by supervising or, if possible, teaching pupils – but such cover will not be provided for teachers who have been absent for three or more consecutive days, and other arrangements, such as the use of supply teachers, will then be made;
(10) participating in arrangements for public examinations;
(11) contributing to management functions including selection of staff, staff development, induction of new staff, coordinating the work of other teachers, etc.;
(12) participating in the administration and organisation of the school, including the ordering and allocation of equipment and materials, attending assemblies, registering and supervising pupils.

Working time is laid down with precision. Full-time teachers are required to be at work for 195 days per annum and on 190 of these days they will teach pupils. The other five days will be devoted to other duties, and some of this time is normally available for in-service training activities. Furthermore, a teacher must work for 1,265 hours a year 'at such times and such places as may be specified by the head teacher'.[11] Teachers should work any additional hours 'as may be needed . . . to discharge effectively professional duties',[12] but the amount of such time required beyond the 1,265 hours is not to be defined by the employer. These new arrangements came into force in August 1987, and from this point teachers in England and Wales moved into a completely new world as far as their employment was concerned. It remains to be seen how these changes will be viewed in the long term, but there can be little doubt that in the context of the 1980s teachers resented having these conditions imposed upon them with minimal consultation. For these reasons, and probably for others as well, the morale of the teaching profession has remained particularly low throughout this period.

Educational expenditure can only take place when funds have been obtained. In the late nineteenth century educational income came from five main sources: (1) donations from private bodies and individuals; (2) endowments and charities; (3) parental fees; (4) central government grants; and (5) local rates. By the second half of the twentieth century the first three of these had lost their importance in the maintained sector and the last two dominated completely. Since the late 1950s the funding of public education has been inextricably bound up with local government finance. It is impossible to understand the former without close study of the latter. Until 1958 the LEAs, which, of course, spent some of their rate income on education, received central government grants from the Ministry of Education specifically earmarked for educational purposes. In that year the whole system of local government was reformed, and the Ministry of Housing and Local Government (later the Department of the Environment) began to pay block grants to local authorities for nearly all their services. Individual authorities were left to decide how they would distribute funds between different services, and from that point educationists had 'to fight their corner' in committee against the needs and demands of other areas of local authority work. At the time there was strong opposition to this change from educational pressure groups such as the Association of Education Committees and the main teachers' unions. As educational expenditure always loomed so large in local authority budgets, there were fears that the new system would lead to retardation in educational expansion, or even to contraction. In the short term these worries proved unfounded, but in the harsher economic climate of the 1970s and 1980s it can be argued that the existence of the block grant system has put considerable added pressure on the education service. In the early 1980s the DES made an attempt to revert to the pre-1958 system of a specific education grant but the Secretary of State, Sir Keith Joseph, was defeated in cabinet committee by the interests of the Department of the Environment.[13]

When the Conservatives came to power in 1979, they made it clear that they believed that excessive public expenditure (including local authority expenditure) was one of the root causes of this country's economic problems. The Government quickly made a firm commitment to contract the public sector. Throughout the 1980s it has been consistently sceptical of the expenditure levels of certain local authorities, regarding them as wasteful and extravagant. The Government also took the view that the existing system of local government finance was too lax and did not control total expenditure sufficiently tightly. To achieve its primary aim of reducing public expenditure, it has been quite prepared to remove local discretion and impose more central control. The Government showed no compunction about shattering assumptions that had been taken for granted in central/local government relations throughout the post-war period. It is now necessary to examine in more detail how local government finance operated at the beginning of the 1980s and how it has been revolutionised in less than a decade.

The system of block grants, refined and entitled Rate Support Grant (RSG) in 1967, remains the basis of central government assistance to local authorities in the 1980s. Each year central government spending departments and the local authority associations negotiate to determine 'relevant expenditure'. This is the total amount of local authority expenditure which central government is prepared to support in the next financial year. The factors taken into consideration in determining relevant expenditure include current expenditure levels, changes in commitments, projected rates of inflation and government economic and expenditure policies. Once the figure of relevant expenditure has been agreed, the Government can announce the level of central support for local authorities it is prepared to meet. For 1987–88 relevant expenditure was agreed at £27,746 million and the Government indicated that it would provide 46.3 per cent (£12,842 million) of this in RSG. Compared with the mid- and late-1970s, 46.3 per cent is a very low proportion. At its peak in 1976 RSG reached 67 per cent and the proportion was still 61 per cent when the Conservatives took office in 1979. The Government has made a conscious political choice and has developed a deliberate policy of reducing this figure year by year. This has meant that the local authorities have had to finance an ever-increasing proportion of the cost of their services out of rates during the 1980s. In these circumstances local authorities have been forced to cut costs (and inevitably to some extent services) and to increase rates. As would be expected, the priorities adopted by different authorities have varied considerably. Few, if any, councils have been able to avoid difficult and painful choices because the proportion of expenditure met by central government grants has fallen so sharply in such a comparatively short period.

The distribution of RSG between different local authorities has an important bearing on the funds available to be spent on services by individual councils. Until 1980 RSG was divided into three parts of which two (resources and needs) effectively determined an authority's share of total RSG. The resources element was designed to 'top up' the low resources of poorer authorities and essentially brought up those councils with low rateable value per head of population to the average national standard. The needs element recognised that there were differences between authorities in their need to spend. There were, for example, variations in age structures of population between authorities, and some councils had to provide for a much greater number of 'expensive' groups such as schoolchildren or senior citizens than others. The needs element tried to take into account a very large number of such factors, but arriving at suitable weightings to reflect the relative importance of all these different factors was an extremely complex and not entirely objective task. The Conservatives were unhappy with the RSG mechanisms and they believed that the needs element was particularly open to criticism. By the late 1970s the needs element was calculated largely by reference to previous levels of spending. This tended to favour previous and current high-spending authorities in the RSG distribution. It perpetuated the status quo, and in many ways ran counter to the Conservatives' desire to restrict local authority public spending.

In 1980 a new system was instituted. The basic aim remained to enable each local authority to provide a standard level of service for the same rate levy in the pound. For the first time, however, each individual authority was given a total expenditure figure which was the Government's assessment of what the authority needed to spend in the year. This figure was called the authority's Grant Related Expenditure (GRE). In the early 1980s, if an authority spent above this figure any extra grant entitlement came to it at a much reduced rate, but soon the system was tightened considerably. The Government began to announce 'targets' as well as GRE (targets were usually somewhat higher than GRE), and if an authority spent more than its target it was subjected to penalties. These penalised an authority with actual grant loss, and in this way it received less central government assistance than it would have done if it had kept its expenditure lower. Assuming that an authority in such a position did not begin to cut services, this grant loss in turn increased its need for even more rate income. In 1986–87 targets and penalties were abolished and replaced by a simpler but equally punitive system. Each authority is now supplied with 'a profile of its grant entitlement at different levels of expenditure'.[14] As expenditure levels increase, the proportion of the cost which will be met from central government grant diminishes, and, if the expenditure level goes beyond a certain point, the authority starts to lose grant. In 1987–88 the Association of County Councils reported that most authorities considered the Government's spending assumptions to be unrealistic.[15] The Association believed that most authorities would find themselves in the position where they began to lose grant as their spending increased, and it is estimated that in 1987–88 £250 million of unclaimed grant would be returned to the Treasury as a result of this.[16] Even the Conservative-controlled Association of County Councils is critical of the grant system that has evolved in the 1980s. It points out that 'creative' accounting techniques have been used to maximise block grant entitlements and that 'budgets and rate levels have been juggled'[17] for similar reasons. Consequently, 'there is no longer a consistent relationship between spending levels and rates' and many authorities opt 'to play the system'.[18] The Association's verdict is clear and worth quoting in full:

'The block grant system was intended to bring local government spending in line with the Government's plans; to ensure a fairer equalisation of needs and resources, and to be more easily understood than the former system. Arguably, none of these objectives has been achieved'.[19]

In the light of the above it is not surprising that those who work in schools and colleges are often confused and confounded by questions of educational and local government finance. It is perhaps now easier for them to appreciate the financial predicament in which local education authorities have been placed throughout most of the last decade.

All local authorities have had to cope with the pressures of the new block grant system in the 1980s, but a minority have also been affected by 'rate capping'. In 1984 the Government took powers to control the maximum rate that could be levied by certain high-spending authorities. The Government was convinced that a relatively small number of councils (probably between fifteen and twenty in most years) was responsible for the national overspend in this area of expenditure. A list of the authorities affected by 'rate capping' is now announced annually. It is claimed by the Government that the pursuit of its overall economic strategy makes it necessary to control total local government expenditure. Its opponents believe that this argument is invalid because public borrowing is not increased by the raising of rates. They see this measure as yet another attempt to reduce local democracy and increase central control. There can be little doubt that, as a result of the Rates Act of 1984, some local authorities (normally Labour-controlled ones) have lost the financial jurisdiction over their own affairs which they had enjoyed since the nineteenth century.

Rates are, of course, alongside central government grant, the local authorities' main source of income. They are essentially an ancient form of local property tax which, during the 1980s, have financed an ever-growing proportion of local authority expenditure. Domestic and non-domestic (industrial, commercial, business, public sector) ratepayers have become increasingly concerned about continual annual rises in their rate bills, and the Thatcher Government has taken interest in their grievances. At the beginning of 1986 a Green Paper entitled *Paying for Local Government*[20] was published, and this contained the basis and justification for changes proposed by the Government. The shortcomings of the rating system have been well known for many years. The problems of adequate property valuation, the difficulties stemming from the fact that rates do not adjust automatically to increases in prices and wages and the regressive nature of the system despite partial alleviation through rate rebate schemes have all been discussed at length in a number of official reports. Over the years there has often been consensus that the rating system had very serious defects, but little progress was made in discussions about what could replace it. Ideas such as a local income tax or a local sales tax have been canvassed, but politicians have not come near to implementing such schemes.

Margaret Thatcher's commitment to abolish domestic rates was put on record as early as 1974, and in *Paying for Local Government* her Government committed itself to this more strongly. In this Green Paper it was stressed that over half the rate income in the country came from the non-domestic sector, and it was pointed out that industry and business (without votes in local elections) had little direct influence over the growth of local authority expenditure and the increase in rate levies. Some Conservatives argued that businesses situated within the boundaries of high-spending authorities were forced to pay a high level of rates which put them at a competitive disadvantage compared with firms from areas with lower rates. It was alleged that, overall, this led to higher levels of unemployment and to relative lack of enterprise in districts controlled by high-spending authorities. In addition, a factor which operated to push up local expenditure was the fact that domestic ratepayers were a much smaller group than those eligible to vote in local elections. Because of rate rebate schemes and other reasons (for example, spouses and adult children of ratepayers still living at home had the vote), only just over half of the electorate in England and Wales was liable to pay rates. It was claimed that all these considerations led to very poor linkage between voting and paying, and that, in practice, local accountability was destroyed by non-ratepayers who voted for higher standards of service without having to count the cost.

In the Local Government Finance Act of 1988 action has been taken to implement the Government's proposals. Domestic rates are to be replaced by a community charge or poll tax. Each local authority will decide on its financial needs, and the resulting charges will be expressed in terms of an amount per head of the adult population. All adults, not just householders, will have to pay this charge, and all local residents will normally face similar bills. It is felt that this method of charging will give all adults a direct incentive to consider costs before they support growth in services involving expenditure. Business rates will pass from the control of local authorities to central government. A uniform countrywide non-domestic rate will be set by Government, and the proceeds from this distributed to local authorities on an adult capitation basis. RSG is to be abolished and superseded by a new Revenue Support Grant. The Secretary of State for the Environment will report to the House of Commons each year on how this grant is to be distributed between authorities, and once parliamentary approval has been given, the distribution will be put into effect. Although the legislation leaves open the principles of distribution which the Secretary of State will take into account when he is considering the Revenue Support Grant, *Paying for Local Government* proposed that a new grant system should contain two elements. Firstly, there was a 'needs' component 'to compensate authorities for differences in the cost of providing a standard level of service to meet local needs', and, secondly, a 'standard' component, which was to be paid on an adult capitation basis, was included 'to produce an equal reduction in the size of the community charge authorities need to levy to finance their spending'.[21] In the early 1990s it will be interesting to find out how the distribution of Revenue Support Grant works out in practice.

The Local Government Finance Act, and particularly the introduction of the community charge or poll tax, is an extremely controversial measure. Although there are exemptions from the charge for some groups (such as those in residential homes) and people on very low incomes are given some financial protection, the poll tax is widely regarded in the country as regressive. The relatively poor in a locality are to be charged just as much as the very rich. Even rates, in a rough and ready fashion, tended to take more from the rich than the poor. During the passage of the Bill even some Conservative members were uneasy about this facet of the poll tax and sought amendments. A few went as far as to vote against the Government, but in the end their revolt made little difference. From the 1990s the vast majority of adults in this country will be required to pay a community charge which will be levied at a flat rate throughout their local area. Duke and dustman will pay the same and their respective incomes will be regarded as irrelevant considerations. It is quite possible that the community charge will succeed in enhancing local accountability. Under the new arrangements electorates could easily prove less willing to support expenditure on local services. Indeed, a £50 increase in annual poll tax will make very little difference to a rich person, but will mean an important reduction in standards of living for a family existing near subsistence level. If these changes persuade electors to seek further cuts in local expenditure at this time, the future for many local education services looks bleak indeed.

During the 1980s a relatively new body, the Manpower Services Commission (MSC) became more and more prominent in educational finance. MSC came into existence at the beginning of 1974 to run training services for adults and school leavers, but, as manufacturing jobs were lost in the early 1980s, it gained greater and greater importance. It worked under the auspices of the Department of Employment and was unconnected with the DES which in itself was significant. During a period in which the LEAs were short of money, the MSC was comparatively richly endowed with resources. Its annual expenditure rose from £640 million in 1978–79 to £3,030 million in 1986–87.[22] MSC had responsibility for developing and financing the Youth Training Scheme (YTS) which grew in importance and size throughout the decade. In 1986–87 the YTS accounted for approximately two-thirds of the MSC's expenditure on vocational education and training programmes. MSC-financed courses now permeated LEA Work-Related Non-Advanced Further Education (WRNAFE) to a considerable extent. From the mid-1980s the Government held back one-quarter of the cost of WRNAFE courses from LEAs and made this money available through MSC. It was argued that this would ensure that courses in further education colleges were kept closely in line with industrial, commercial and business needs and were linked closely with national and local employment opportunities. Although this change in financial control was opposed by the LEAs and the further education teachers at the time, they have had to learn to live and work with MSC funding and control. The Government has also financed its major initiative for the education and training of 14–18 year olds through the MSC. This measure, the Technical and Vocational Education Initiative (TVEI), brought the MSC into contact with secondary schools. Although LEAs did not like the MSC entering what they saw as their prime territory, TVEI was by far the most important innovation in the secondary curriculum during the 1980s and they found it difficult to ignore the funds that were being made available. At first some LEAs refused to take part in the scheme, but as TVEI was extended (eventually it will be available in all secondary schools) these have come into line. At the same time MSC has retained major responsibility for the organisation and funding of a wide range of programmes for the training and re-training of adults, and at present its role and influence in higher education is being developed at a fast rate. There can be little doubt that the emergence of the MSC has been one of the most important changes in education and training in the 1980s. MSC has achieved its current position of influence and status, at least in part, because it has had a relatively large and growing budget when its potential rivals in the field, particularly the LEAs, have been short of money. In 1988 the MSC was renamed the Training Commission, and, after the Trades Union Congress withdrew its support for the Employment Training Programme, it was abolished and its functions performed directly by the Department of Employment. It is now known as the Training Agency.

The rise of the MSC and the increased control exercised by the Treasury and the Department of the Environment has left the DES with a much-reduced influence over the service which it in name administers. In order to try to develop some scope for DES initiatives in the system, central government education support grants were introduced in 1985. One per cent of planned local authority expenditure on education is currently deducted from RSG and put at the disposal of the DES. The Department asks local authorities to make bids for this money but specifies in some detail the purposes for which these grants can be used. Local authorities tend to take the view that they are being required to bid to get back their own money, and it is important to realise that education support grants do not put extra resources into the service. They are essentially a means of giving the DES an opportunity to specify and control a number of national spending priorities. The introduction of the education support grant system has further reduced the financial discretion of LEAs, but in this case, rather unusually, the increase in central control was taken by the DES. More typically, as LEAs have lost influence over funding in the 1980s, the initiative has passed to other government departments, especially to Environment and, through the MSC, to Employment.

In its endeavour to help local authorities to provide their services economically, efficiently and effectively the Government set up the Audit Commission in 1982. This body has since carried out a number of inquiries into aspects of the management of education and has produced several influential reports including *Aspects of Non-Teaching Costs in Secondary Schools* (1984),[23] *Obtaining Better Value for Further Education* (1985)[24] and *Towards Better Management of Secondary Education* (1986).[25] Emphasis is placed on eliminating waste and ensuring that ratepayers receive maximum value for money. With the same ends in mind in recent years private firms of management consultants have also been commissioned to investigate certain educational questions. In 1988, for example, Coopers and Lybrand Associates reported to the DES on the *Local Management of Schools*[26] and Deliotte, Haskins and Sells Management Consultancy Division produced a consultation document for the MSC on *The Funding of Vocational Education and Training*.[27] There can be little doubt that one of the main purposes of this new trend is to make professional educators (both administrators and teachers) question their usual assumptions and their established procedures. It is intended that education should become more 'money conscious' and generally feel the pressures experienced daily in the private sector. Few would wish to deny the need for effective and efficient use of resources in education, but there are some who would push things further believing that education has been cocooned for too long and requires a 'good shake out'. It is likely that both of these viewpoints are reflected in the recent spate of reports on management, particularly financial management, of the education service.

There is no doubt that central government has tightened its financial controls over local authorities considerably during the 1980s, but now LEAs will soon be faced with the Government's plans for greater financial delegation to schools. The Government

believes that the governors and head teachers of schools should
be given more freedom to decide their own expenditure priorities
and should see their own school reap the benefit if any savings
are made through greater efficiency. For many years schools have
normally controlled the expenditure from their annual capitation
allowances, and from September 1987 LEAs have been required
by law to give schools a lump sum to spend on books, equipment
and stationery. In some authorities school governors and heads
have been given responsibility for much larger budgets, and it is
well known that the then Secretary of State, Kenneth Baker, took a
strong interest in the experiments in school financial management
tried in Cambridgeshire and Solihull.

In the 1988 Education Reform Act schools and further education colleges are given responsibility for their own budgets. LEAs
are required to produce schemes of financial delegation and to
submit them to the Secretary of State for approval. Circular 7/88
sets out the details of what is required in these local schemes
including the important provision that at least 75 per cent of the
funds available to schools should be allocated on the basis of the
numbers of pupils and their ages. Governors will receive the
responsibility for expenditure on a wide range of items including
repairs and staffing. LEAs will retain control of capital
expenditure, school transport, the advisory and welfare services.
Governing bodies will have much more influence over levels of
staffing than before, and they will be able, for example, either to
take on an extra teacher or to spend funds on additional
secretarial help, more books and materials. The particular mix
will be determined at the school level by the governors normally ac-
ting with the advice of the head teacher. Although LEAs will
continue to employ teachers, many staffing matters will be
devolved to governing bodies. They will have the major responsibility for selecting teachers and for their promotion. It will
become more difficult for LEAs to move teachers from one
school to another, and governors will not be obliged to take a
teacher they do not want. If a governing body wishes to reduce
the number of teachers in its school and contemplates making an
individual redundant, it will notify the LEA which will be obliged
to give that teacher notice of dismissal. Clearly, once these
measures are implemented, governors and heads will have much
greater roles in management and will need considerable expertise
in handling financial affairs. This is acknowledged by the Government, and it is intended that the training for governors and head
teachers required by the 1986 Education Act will be extended to
include financial management techniques.

In their report *Local Management of Schools*[28] Coopers and
Lybrand make several important points about financial delegation
to schools. They stress that there will be a need for a new kind

of school governor, and that the success or failure of the scheme will depend crucially on head teachers and their senior colleagues in schools. Heads and deputies will have a considerable number of new administrative burdens placed upon them, and it remains to be seen whether they will be able to cope with these in addition to the onerous and important duties that they already perform. Coopers and Lybrand argue that financial delegation will not be cheap and they doubt whether savings will accrue even in the long run. It is important that those with political power recognise this and do not see these changes as yet another opportunity to cut costs. Coopers and Lybrand acknowledge quite openly that greater economies of scale can be achieved in a more centralised system, for example, a large LEA using central purchasing can normally obtain bigger discounts than individual schools. In general, however, they support financial delegation, believing that it should enable schools to adjust more flexibly to day-to-day requirements and to changing needs. Above all it should provide incentives for teachers and governors to use resources as efficiently and as economically as possible and thereby reap financial benefits for their own institution. It will be interesting to observe how financial delegation works out in practice in the 1990s.

Throughout the 1980s this country has had a government which has been continually suspicious of local authorities and particularly sceptical of the costs of the services which they provide. At the same time it has been a great admirer of the discipline imposed by market forces and by the achievements of the private sector in the economy. These attitudes have coloured its views on educational finance. As early as 1980 it introduced the Assisted Places Scheme which provided the means for intelligent children from less wealthy homes to attend independent schools. This transferred pupils and resources from the local authority to the private sector at a point when cuts were already being imposed on the former. In many ways it set the tone for the decade. Later, in 1986, the Government announced that it intended to develop City Technology Colleges which were to break the local authority monopoly of free secondary education in urban areas. It hoped that private sponsors would come forward and share the capital costs of these institutions, but the Government must have been disappointed by the private sector's limited response to this venture. Nonetheless, those who work in schools, colleges and universities know that emphasis is now regularly placed on raising as much as possible from private firms and individuals, because income from public funds looks less secure and, in real terms, is much less generous than it used to be. The present trend indicates that it is almost certain that dependence on private funding may become even more important during the 1990s.

The promotion of the private sector, the development of a

central agency for providing training schemes, the privatisation of school meals, cleaning and ground maintenance in many areas, the now extensive controls exercised by central government over local expenditure and the changes outlined in the 1988 Education Reform Act and the Local Government Finance Act make the outlook for LEAs particularly bleak. During the 1980s one of the principle means employed to reduce their influence was to tamper with and to erode their financial base. It may be that this country can operate a successful education service without LEAs, but, as yet, there are no plans for their abolition. In the 1990s it is clear that central government, individual institutions and private firms will hold the purse strings with LEAs effectively reduced to a subsidiary role as intermediate agents operating between the other parties. It is possible that this will produce a more divisive education system than we have become accustomed to in the second half of the twentieth century. If, at any point, there is a desire to counter this, it will be an urgent necessity to reconstruct the financial base of LEAs as quickly as possible.

REFERENCES

1. DES 1987 Statistical Bulletin 14/87 HMSO, December.
2. The Treasury, HMSO Economic Progress Report 189, The Budget, HMSO March/April.
3. DES, *op cit.*
4. P. Gosden 1985 Education Policy 1979–84, in D. Bell (ed.) *The Conservative Government 1979–84, An Interim Report,* Croom Helm, pp. 111–12.
5. DES, *op cit.,*
6. DES, 1987 *Teachers' Pay and Conditions. A Consultative Document,* HMSO, p. 7
7. *Ibid.,* p. 31
8. DES, 1987 *School Teachers' Pay and Conditions Document,* HMSO.
9. *Ibid.,* p. 25.
10. *Ibid.,* pp. 23–5.
11. *Ibid.,* p. 25.
12. *Ibid.,* pp. 25–6.
13. P. Gosden, *op. cit.,* p. 118.
14. Association of County Councils, 1987 *Understanding Block Grants 1987–88* p. 11.
15. *Ibid.,* p. 13.
16. *Ibid.*
17. *Ibid.,* p. 19.
18. *Ibid.*
19. *Ibid.*
20. Department of Environment, 1986 *Paying for Local Government,* HMSO.

21. *Ibid.*, p. 34.
22. Manpower Services Commission, 1981–82 and 1986–87 *Annual Reports*.
23. Audit Commission, 1984 *Obtaining Better Value in Education: Aspects of Non-Teaching Costs in Secondary Schools*.
24. Audit Commission, 1985 *Obtaining Value for Further Education*.
25. Audit Commission, 1986 *Towards Better Management of Secondary Education*.
26. Coopers and Lybrand Associates, 1987 *Local Management of Schools: Report to the DES*, Coopers and Lybrand.
27. Deloitte, Haskins and Sells (Management Consultancy Division) 1987 *The Funding of Vocational Education and Training: Report to Manpower Sources Commission*.
28. Coopers and Lybrand Associates, *op. cit.*

FURTHER READING

Coopers and Lybrand Associates 1987 *Local Management of Schools: Report to the DES*, Coopers and Lybrand.
Deloitte, Haskins and Sells 1987 *The Funding of Vocational Education and Training: Report to the MSC*, Manpower Services Commission.
Dennison, W. F. 1984 *Educational Finance and Resources*, Croom Helm.
DES 1987 *Teachers' Pay and Conditions. A Consultative Document*, HMSO.
DES (latest edition available) *School Teachers' Pay and Conditions Document*, HMSO.
Department of Environment 1986 *Paying for Local Government*, HMSO.

CHAPTER 6

Education and training for those over 16 years of age

The range of education and training activities considered in this chapter will be very wide. Not only the courses but also the institutions which provide them are varied and disparate. In this area it is particularly difficult to detect much overall planning and coherence. What is now available is largely a reflection of the historical development of institutions set up at various times to serve different and sometimes distinct purposes without much reference to what already existed and to what was already going on in neighbouring fields. The scope of the chapter extends from the YTS scheme to Oxbridge, but, as the former makes an impact on far more of our citizens than the latter, it will receive greater attention.

Many secondary schools are, of course, involved in the education of post-16 pupils. Since the days of Arnold at Rugby, secondary schools have traditionally prized their sixth forms. Until the mid-1970s school sixth forms were predominantly places where students followed three (occasionally four) academic 'A' level courses normally in closely related subjects. The assumption often was, and sometimes still is, that the majority of sixth formers were preparing themselves for entry to higher education, in most cases to take honours degree courses at universities. Although in some instances provisions were offered for re-sit 'O' level candidates, before the 1970s comparatively little provision was made in school sixth forms for students who required and wanted one-year courses which were preparatory to entering employment. From the mid-1970s comprehensive schools became increasingly involved in the provision of pre-vocational courses such as those offered by the Royal Society of Arts (RSA), City and Guilds of London Institute (CGLI) and the Business and Technician Education Council (BTEC). This theme will be taken up in more detail later in the chapter. The development of comprehensive schools in the 1960s and 1970s has led to the wider dispersal of sixth-form students between schools. There are more comprehensive schools than there were grammar schools, and despite the increased tendency to stay at school beyond 16, there has been a reduction in average sixth-form size. In the 1980s a smaller age cohort and falling school rolls have further exacerbated this situation. It is estimated that the 16–19-year-old population in England will fall from a peak of 2.4 million in 1983 to a trough of 1.6 million in 1995, representing a reduction of one-third,[1] and it is clear that existing trends affecting sixth-form size will continue. These factors have already led to acute problems in some schools. 'A' level courses in a number of minority subjects are no longer viable in a growing proportion of schools. To replicate provisions for small groups of 'A' level students (or for that matter for other activities) in schools in close proximity in the same city or town is clearly wasteful in the use of scarce human and material resources. In some instances there is evidence that, in order to preserve sixth-form options, particularly in minority 'A' level subjects, the allocation of staff in some schools is quite disproportionate. Such misallocation of staffing can lead to situations where the quality of education for pupils under 16 can suffer, because staffing the small sixth-form groups means that pupil–teacher ratios for classes of younger children have to be kept higher than they otherwise would have been. The DES has also made the important point that sixth-form teaching groups need to be of sufficient size to provide the necessary educational stimulation.[2]

Many LEAs have been aware of these issues for some considerable time and have tried to reorganise their sixth-form provisions accordingly. In some districts consortia involving several secondary schools have been arranged for sixth-form work. Standard subjects are available on each site in the grouping, but a particular minority interest will only be catered for at one of the schools in the consortium. This helps to keep teaching group sizes viable, but can involve complex timetables and travelling arrangements. It is also claimed that students working under such conditions can live a transient existence, losing a clear sense of identification with a particular school. The DES believes that experience has shown that consortium-type arrangements are difficult to operate successfully in practice.[3] 'Mushroom' sixth forms have been created in other areas. In this form of organisation secondary schools are grouped with a single school retaining pupils over the age of 16. The other schools in the group continue to educate only pre-16 pupils and they transfer their students who wish to continue their education beyond the minimum leaving age to the institution which retains its sixth form. It can be difficult to establish 'parity of esteem' between the different schools in such a grouping. Often parents see thè school with the sixth form as the 'best' and the others as distinctly 'second best'. In such a situation there is frequently competition between parents to obtain places in the school with the sixth form for their children at the minimum age of entry (normally 11 or 12) and some reluctance to use the other schools.

The DES has seen and acknowledged the need to rationalise

the provision of sixth-form places at a time of falling rolls. When it issued *Better Schools*[4] and later a draft circular in 1986, it suggested that a comprehensive school required a sixth form in the order of 150 students 'to sustain its educational viability at an acceptable cost'.[5] Although this figure was not mentioned in the definitive version (Circular 3/87, *Providing for Quality: The Pattern of Organisation to Age 19*), it was emphasised that, 'A school sixth form can be expected, not least by parents and students, to offer a choice of 'A' level subjects which include all those commonly taken and an appropriate selection of other subjects. Such an approach would normally lead to a choice of not less than about 15 subjects.'[6] The Circular continued, stating that there were 'strong educational advantages in securing teaching groups of not less than an average of 10 students',[7] although it was acknowledged that smaller numbers might be unavoidable to preserve a minority subject or introduce a new one. These criteria continue to discourage, but do not absolutely rule out, small sixth forms in comprehensive schools. In 1982 the then Secretary of State, Sir Keith Joseph, made it clear that he would not normally approve reorganisation schemes which involved the closure of or significant changes to the character of schools of 'proven worth'.[8] One of the touchstones of 'proven worth' was 'a sustained record of success in the provision (made) for sixth-form education'.[9] This has offered schools with small but successful (usually assessed in terms of examination results in academic subjects) sixth forms some considerable protection from reorganisation. It will continue to do so unless it can be shown that in a particular case a school will no longer be able 'to sustain its established quality' or that 'alternative proposals would secure the same quality and variety of education at lower cost'.[10] The DES has asked LEAs to review their total provisions for 16–19 education (further education and sixth-form colleges as well as schools) and 'to take appropriate action in the interest of good education and economy'.[11] They are specifically requested to have regard to the cost and the disruption that changes will involve, but the Secretary of State has indicated that he has 'no preferred solution to the outcome of the review'. School sixth forms of various kinds, further education colleges, sixth form colleges and tertiary colleges are all acceptable forms of organisation to central government. During the 1990s it will be interesting to see whether major changes take place or whether the status quo prevails. For a time during 1985 and 1986 it appeared that the DES was prepared to support, even encourage, some radical reorganisation in this area, but the more recent indications of 1987 and 1988 point to the preservation of well-established institutions, such as the school sixth form, widely throughout the education system.

Several LEAs have developed sixth-form colleges in recent years. The first was set up in Luton in 1966 and several followed a year later in Hampshire. In 1987 there were 106 sixth-form colleges in 44 LEAs and over 20 per cent of all students in the 16–19 age range in the schools' sector attended them.[12] Their average size was under 600 students. Nearly all sixth-form colleges offer a broad range of 'A' level subjects and very many also put on a selection of non-academic courses. These colleges do not operate under the DES's further education provisions but are controlled by schools regulations. This has important ramifications as these colleges are not normally permitted to enrol part-time students or those over 19 years of age. Their teachers are paid on the schoolteachers' scale and they are normally members of the schoolteacher unions. Sixth-form colleges co-exist alongside further education colleges, and there is in some districts competition between these rivals for certain students such as those wanting 'A' level courses. Falling rolls continue to increase the pressure to reorganise sixth forms. Although some educators see the future in terms of combining further education provisions and sixth forms into tertiary colleges, others are sceptical of this radical solution. Some parents, who during the late 1980s are receiving some support from certain influential quarters in the Conservative Party, maintain that academic 'A' level students should not be mixed with those on vocational courses and day-release trainees. If this view prevails, it is likely that the number of sixth-form colleges will increase significantly in the 1990s. It is already clear that several LEAs are devising reorganisation schemes which include the introduction and development of sixth-form colleges.

In contrast to sixth-form colleges, tertiary colleges work under further education regulations. As has been mentioned in Chapter 1, the origins of the further education service are to be found in the second half of the nineteenth century. For much of this century further education has been associated in the public mind with the local municipal technical college, and although this was essentially correct in an earlier period, such an association now considerably understates the range and heterogeneous nature of the courses and services available in the further education sector. In 1986 there were 322,000 enrolments on full-time (including sandwich) Non-Advanced Further Education (NAFE) courses in maintained colleges. In addition, there were no fewer than 1,279,000 enrolments on part-time courses and 119,000 YTS students attending colleges.[13] The DES expects total enrolments to increase very slightly by 1994, but it believes that there will be changes in the pattern of attendance with the result that the number of full-time equivalent students will fall in the early 1990s.[14] It predicts that the age structure of NAFE students will also change with fewer 16–18-year-olds and more aged over 25.

Those who have derived their image of further education from Tom Sharpe's novel *Wilt*[15] and the infamous *Meat One* need to update their picture. The typical further education student, if there ever was one, is no longer a white male apprentice on day release. Changes in manufacturing industry in the 1980s have led to a drastic decline in the number of apprenticeships available. Although long-established examining bodies such as the City and Guilds of London Institute (CGLI) with their qualifications in technical and industrial subjects and the Royal Society of Arts (RSA) with their courses in commercial and office studies are still important in further education, new bodies have also emerged. In the 1970s the Business Education Council (BEC) and the Technician Education Council (TEC) were created and their awards replaced qualifications such as the old ordinary and higher national certificates and diplomas. In 1983 BEC and TEC merged to form the Business and Technician Education Council (BTEC) which now controls a large range of awards for industry, agriculture, commerce and finance, information technology, distributive and leisure services and public administration. Although these changes made considerable impact on the further education service, they were not as influential as the most basic alterations brought about by the emergence of the Training Agency, formerly the Manpower Services Commission (MSC).

For many years industrial training was mainly the responsibility of employers and took place 'on the job'. Although there were often opportunities to attend day-release classes at the local technical college, young, especially male, workers learned their skills in the workplace through the apprenticeship system. Some firms invested in training, but others took this issue insufficiently seriously, sometimes preferring to poach trained skilled workers from their competitors. In 1964 the Industrial Training Act set up boards to control training in most sectors of industry. These industrial training boards could impose levies on employers in their sector to finance their activities. By the 1970s there were doubts about the effectiveness of some of the industrial training boards and there was still some feeling in industrial and political circles that this country was not meeting its training needs for the future. As a result in 1973 the Employment and Training Act was passed. This set up the Manpower Services Commission and in the longer term most of the industrial training boards were phased out. The MSC consisted of ten commissioners who were appointed by the Secretary of State for Employment after consultation with the Confederation of British Industry (three members), the Trades Union Congress (three members), the local authority associations (two members) and the professional education associations (one member). The Chair was independent of these interest groups. The Commission was given wide powers to promote training schemes and to provide employment services. It worked under the auspices of the Department of Employment, but from 1977 the MSC's activities in Wales came under the ministerial responsibility of the Secretary of State for Wales. In 1988 the MSC was retitled the Training Commission, but, when the Trades Union Congress withdrew its support from the new Employment Training programme for unemployed adults, the Government took the view that the commission, which included three representatives from the TUC, was unworkable. No further meetings of the Training Commission were held and from the autumn of 1988 this body became known as the Training Agency. Its functions, at least for the time being, are performed directly by the Department of Employment.

During the 1970s the MSC initiated a number of schemes, but these have now been overshadowed by those of the 1980s, especially the Youth Training Scheme (YTS). The considerable rise in unemployment, particularly youth unemployment, in the late 1970s and 1980s, enhanced the role of the MSC in the economy and society. Table 6.1 illustrates how drastically the position of young people changed in just over a decade.[16]

TABLE 6.1
Educational and economic activities of 16-years-olds 1975–86 (Great Britain)

	% 1975	% 1986
School	26	30
Full-time FE College	11	15
Employment	61	19
Youth Training Scheme	–	26
Unemployed	2	10

Towards the end of 1981 the now famous 'New Training Initiative'[17] was launched. It stressed that apprenticeship was in decline although it failed to mention that one of the basic causes of this was the contraction in British manufacturing industry. It also pointed out that training opportunities for young people on the continent were more widely taken up than in this country. In future all unemployed 16-year-old school leavers were to be offered a one-year traineeship and some older school leavers were also eligible to join the scheme. Trainees were to receive an allowance, and their training was to take place primarily 'on the job' although each trainee was guaranteed a minimum of thirteen weeks 'off the job' training as well. Young people in employment could be included in the scheme as long as their employers undertook to provide the necessary training opportunities. Training content was to include five main elements: (1) induction, (2) basic skills including numeracy, literacy and communication, (3) personal and occupational skills adapted to meet the needs of a variety of work contexts and the local labour market, (4) guidance and counselling and (5) record and review of progress. Most trainees worked on schemes controlled by managing agents who were paid for designing and delivering whole training programmes. In some instances where there was a shortfall in places or where there were difficulties in finding opportunities for particular groups of youngsters, MSC arranged with voluntary organisations to provide training in special workshops, on community projects or bought places on courses in colleges. The Commission has always stressed that it prefers the former arrangements to the latter, and it has tried to reduce the number of places in the latter category as much as it can. Industrial and commerical firms in the private sector are used as much as possible, and, to try to institute quality control more effectively, from 1988 only 'approved training organisations' which meet specified criteria were utilised. It is hoped that this will help to reduce the number of accusations that allege that some firms are more interested in receiving free labour than in providing stimulating and worthwhile training opportunities. In 1986 the YTS was extended to two years so that trainees were able to seek and obtain recognised vocational qualifications within their period on the scheme. This has broadened the scope of the original initiative in a significant manner at the same time as it has doubled the length of the period of monitored training. By the late 1980s YTS had become a most important, almost the standard, route into employment for school leavers. Many believe that, in effect. YTS has now replaced apprenticeship, and that it provides training opportunities for a much wider group of young people than apprenticeship ever did. On the other hand, those young people who complete their YTS successfully but who do not find employment must never be forgotten.

The MSC's influence was extended after 1984 by the implementation of government policy set out in *Training for Jobs*.[18] Considerable emphasis was placed in this document on the importance of vocationalism in schools and colleges. YTS and TVEI were hailed as great successes, but it was emphasised that much still had to be done. It was claimed:

Successful training is a continuing investment in the most valuable of all our national resources – the energies of our people. We have not sufficiently recognised its importance in the past. This we must now remedy and ensure that the skills of our people are fitted for the challenge of the years ahead. . . . Public sector provision for training and vocational education must become more responsive to employment needs at national and local level. The public sector needs a greater incentive to relate the courses it provides more clearly to the needs of the customer and in the most cost effective way. . . The Manpower Services Commission is now the main agency through which the government institutes action and monitors progress in training.[19]

Training for Jobs proposed to transfer one-quarter of the cost of Work Related Non-Advanced Further Education (WRNAFE) from Rate Support Grant paid to LEAs to the MSC. The reaction from both Labour and Conservative LEAs was hostile. They resented the fact that this proposal was announced without any consultations whatsoever. They held that the implicit allegations that their further education courses were unresponsive to employment needs and were not cost effective were unsubstantiated. They also believed, with some justification, that employers were far from clear in their own minds about what their training requirements were. Tom King, Secretary of State for Employment, did not help matters when he said that 'previous training for jobs had been handled in a haphazard and inadequate way',[20] but in the mid-1980s the further education sector took great pains to show how it was responsive to the needs of employers and to define and analyse cost effectiveness with a view to improvement. At first it looked as if *Training for Jobs* would be implemented over the heads of the LEAs with bids having to be made to the MSC for each and every WRNAFE course. Compromise was reached, however, and it was agreed that LEAs would draw up development plans for WRNAFE jointly with MSC officials thus allowing colleges to retain some control over their courses. In many ways, in the longer term, this new system did not lead to the conflict that was anticipated, but its introduction marked a considerable reduction in LEA, and for that matter DES, influence over vocational education and training in this country. The further education sector may not yet be completely reconciled to working under the Training Agency (formerly MSC), but, in practice, it knows that for the foreseeable future it will continue to do so. In its annual report MSC took the view that the planning arrangements for WRNAFE introduced in 1986 had operated effectively. It believed that the new system 'had a marked effect on the way LEAs arranged provision'.[21] Employer involvement was more active, better management information systems were introduced and marketing was improved. It claimed that these views were supported by Deloitte, Haskins and Sells' independent surveys *The Funding of Vocational Education and Training*[22] and by the HMI report, *NAFE in Practice*.[23]

This brief account of the MSC has concentrated on only two

of its activities – YTS and WRNAFE. The MSC, of course, encompassed a much wider range of services than this. It financed, for example, a large number of training and retraining schemes for unemployed adults which cannot be mentioned here. It was also concerned with curriculum development in secondary schools with its Technical and Vocational Educational Initiative (TVEI) for 14–18-year-old pupils, and information technology centres and the open tech programmes operated under its auspices. The emergence of the MSC (later the Training Commission then the Training Agency) must rank as one of the most important developments in the education and training system in the 1980s. It quickly established a reputation for getting its own way and for delivering the goods. It became a most influential and powerful body. It could not have achieved this status and importance without help from its friends holding high political offices who endowed it with relatively generous finances when other bodies in the education service were short of money.

Late in 1988 the Government issued a white paper entitled *Employment for the 1990s*[24] which contained proposals for completely new structures for vocational training in this country. The Training Commission will be formally abolished, and in future advice to government at the national level will be provided by a new body, the National Training Task Force. This will consist of twelve members, two-thirds of whom will be leaders from industry and commerce. In the localities, one hundred Training and Enterprise Councils (TECs) will be established. At least two-thirds of the places on these councils will be given to local employers. It is expected that in many areas the TECs will be built around the chambers of commerce. Their main functions will be to examine and support local training programmes for young people (mainly YTS) and for adults. The TECs will not undertake training themselves, but, having assessed changing local needs, will contract out programmes to managing agents who will actually operate the schemes. This proposed new framework underlines the predominant position of employers in training and weakens still further the roles of the trade unions and the further education service.

The development of the MSC in the 1980s was a prime example of the Thatcher Governments' attraction to centralist solutions to the problems encountered in the education and training field. This non-elected body was given a wide remit and, by the standards of the 1980s, generous funding. It is now to be replaced by non-elected local TECs which will be dominated by employers. These new councils, however, will be centrally funded on a contract basis through the Department of Employment's Training Agency. It will be interesting to see whether these new bodies manage to enhance the effectiveness of vocational training in this country. There is wide agreement that Britain, unlike many of its competitors, has failed in this area over a long period and that this issue is vitally important. The country is now being led to believe that the Training Agency with its TECs will be able to make an active, positive contribution to sustained economic recovery in the 1990s. Faith has been placed in a relatively narrow partnership between central government and employers, with other interest groups largely excluded. It is frequently alleged that the wider partnerships of the past have failed to deliver what was necessary; central government and employers must now quickly demonstrate that this privatisation of training can work effectively in practice.

Both further education colleges and schools have been affected by the emphasis on vocationalism exemplified by the rise and development of the Training Agency. Important curriculum developments which fall outside the scope of this body have also been similarly influenced during the 1980s. For some years it was clear that there were many sixteen-year-olds who wanted a further year of full-time education after the minimum leaving age but who were uninterested in and unsuitable for 'A' level courses. In the 1970s schools and colleges tried to accommodate an increasing number of such students by fitting them into existing examination structures and they were largely provided with a diet of re-sit 'O' levels. This was unsatisfactory for the majority of these students. They found repeating material which they had already failed in the fifth form boring and soul-destroying and, understandably, the failure rate for re-sit 'O' levels was high. Educationists increasingly took the view that these students should be encouraged to look forward to and prepare for the world after school and college rather than reflect on the failings of an unsuccessful time in the fourth and fifth forms.

In schools a new Certificate of Extended Education (CEE) was introduced. This was school-subject based and students were normally assessed in five subjects at the age of 17. Schools had considerable freedom over syllabus content and methods of assessment and they were able to adapt subjects to meet the perceived needs of their own pupils. Content was often made relevant to the world of work and vocational elements introduced where appropriate. At the same time rather different developments were taking place in the further education sector. The City and Guilds of London Institute (CGLI), a long-established provider of courses in technical subjects, began to offer courses that were much more specifically pre-vocational in their orientation than CEE. Its foundation courses, which were focused on groups of related industries, aimed at helping students make more informed vocational choices. It also launched a general vocational preparation course, which proved particularly popular. The Royal Society of Arts (RSA) entered the field with general pre-employment courses for clerical and office work and in skills required in personal services and the distributive trades. These courses made an impact on schools as well as on further education with the CGLI's general course making the greatest inroads. Often link courses between schools and some of the more specialised further education institutions such as building or catering colleges were organised so that pupils could gain access to the specialist equipment and staff located there. Pupils and students were increasingly involved in periods of work experience.

At the end of the 1970s the developments in CEE and the FE vocational preparation courses were reviewed in separate official reports. It was agreed that there was an urgent need for new provisions for 16–17-year-olds of average and less than average ability, and that courses for this group should be vocationally orientated, helping them 'to understand what employers would expect from them and what they should expect from employment'. The school-focused report, however, recommended the continuation of CEE on the basis of individual subjects with assessment culminating in examinations. The FE report, which was entitled *A Basis for Choice*,[25] favoured a common core of vocational preparation with profile assessment and records of achievement rather than examinations. It did not want the course divided into subject components and proposed a core curriculum 'framework' or 'structure' of pre-vocational studies rather than a syllabus in the conventional sense.

After these reports were published, there was a power struggle between the interest groups involved. The CSE boards, the Schools Council and the schoolteacher unions all supported the CEE-type approach, and the FE institutions and teachers proclaimed the virtues of *A Basis for Choice*. Eventually the Government came out in favour of *A Basis for Choice*, which has proved to be a most influential document. From this a new course and qualification, the Certificate of Pre-Vocational Education (CPVE), was developed in the mid-1980s. It is available in both schools and FE colleges, and now forms an important part of the Government's training strategy. When it was launched, it was given wide publicity and strong support from ministerial level. Important links with some YTS schemes have already been developed, and some believe that CPVE should eventually become the standard first year of the two-year YTS.

CPVE is controlled by a Joint Board for Pre-Vocational Education set up by BTEC and CGLI. Like *A Basis for Choice*, CPVE is a framework rather than a course with syllabus content prescribed. It is taken by students with a wide range of abilities.

The CPVE framework includes a common core of skills that are needed in adult life and can be applied in a variety of employment situations. Students, in addition, are helped to develop their interests and skills in one or more of five specified vocational areas. All schemes are required to have at least fifteen days' work experience, and assessment is based on 'a continuous collection of statements about a student's competence'. Individual counselling and guidance form an important part of the course, and there is an expectation of considerable discussion and negotiation between a student and a tutor about the individual's programme of work. During the course CPVE students build up portfolios of work and profiles are kept which contain information about achievements and capabilities. There is often considerable emphasis on job seeking and enterprise skills, and sometimes students are involved in setting up and running their own mini-businesses.

Much space has been devoted to CPVE and its evolution because it represents a radical development in education which, in many ways, is typical of the 1980s. If the new approaches adopted by CPVE, and they are not unlike those also being taken up in TVEI, prove successful in the long term, it is possible that they will be the harbingers of major changes at the level of practice throughout this country's education service. It is an irony, not unnoticed by many teachers and lecturers, that it is during a period of high youth unemployment that more stress has been placed on vocational and pre-vocational education than ever before.

Another innovation of the 1980s which has affected, at least potentially, the education of 16–19-year-olds is the introduction of Advanced/Supplementary (AS) levels. These were first offered in September 1987. Schools and colleges are not obliged to enter this new field although they have been encouraged to do so, and, similarly, students can stay with well-established 'A' level courses if they so desire. Syllabuses for AS levels contain approximately half the content of equivalent 'A' levels but they are intended to reflect the same standard of achievement. The main purpose of introducing AS levels was to encourage students to be less specialised in their 16–19 courses. There was considerable concern, for example, that Science and Mathematics students gave up modern languages completely and that Arts-based 'A' level candidates were sometimes innumerate, having dropped Mathematics and Science from their studies. It was hoped that some students might be persuaded to take two 'A' levels and two 'AS' levels, preferably in contrasting subjects instead of the usual three 'A' levels. The introduction of AS levels was welcomed by the teaching profession and, according to the DES, by employers. Higher education institutions have supported this development and in principle they are prepared to accept these new qualifications for entry purposes. In practice, however, entry to higher education is controlled by individual departments in universities and colleges and it still remains to be seen whether they will be conservative with regard to their own entry requirements. Some students in schools and colleges are being advised to bear this consideration in mind before committing themselves to the new AS courses.

The Government encouraged examination boards, schools and colleges to give priority to devising AS courses and syllabuses in Mathematics, Science, Design/Technology, French, English and General Studies. During 1987–88 about 15 per cent of the schools with 'A' level pupils mounted AS courses, and the Secretary of State expected that three times as many would do so in 1988–89. AS levels have been introduced at a time when schools and colleges have been under considerable financial strain, and it has not been easy to provide either the necessary new books and equipment or the staffing. During 1988 the Government indicated that it attached considerable importance to the role of AS levels in broadening the sixth-form curriculum, and it ruled out, at least in the short term, some rather more radical proposals as will be explained below. If AS levels are to be successful in this, they will require the interest and support of the full range of educational institutions operating in the field. If, for example, certain well-known university departments or leading independent schools choose to ignore AS levels, it is not likely that any impact will be made on the traditional, perhaps ossified sixth-form curriculum.

The Thatcher Government is firmly committed to retaining 'A' levels as they are regarded as 'an essential means for setting standards of excellence'.[26] In March 1987 the Higginson Committee was set up to consider 'A' level syllabuses and their assessment. The report of the Committee was published in June 1988[27] and immediately provoked controversy. Higginson's aims were to increase the breadth in the programmes of study for 'A' level students and to make these programmes more suitable for a wider range of students. The Committee recommended that a new five-subject 'A' level system should be introduced in the 1990s with Arts-based students encouraged to take at least one Science, and vice versa. It believed that time could be found for five subjects if syllabuses were made leaner and superfluous factual material, which was often merely memorised by candidates, was removed. In the new 'A' level system subjects would be allocated six periods per week instead of the eight normally given at present. The Higginson recommendations received strong support from the teachers, higher education, industry, business and commerce, but within minutes they were turned down by the

Secretary of State. It was indicated that the report had been rejected for three main reasons. Firstly, a new 'A' level system could easily 'queer the pitch' for AS levels which were already up and running and increasingly acceptable for entry to higher education. Secondly, ministers were not convinced that syllabuses could be made leaner and tougher without diluting rigour and lowering academic standards. Thirdly, teachers, parents and pupils already had to cope with the introduction of GCSE, the National Curriculum and testing at 7, 11, 14 and 16 and other items in the 1988 Education Reform Act. The Government felt that the education service would be 'overloaded' if further changes were planned for the early 1990s. There is evidence, however, that this is only part of the story. Publication of the report was delayed for several weeks, and leaks have suggested that it was the Prime Minister, whose commitment to traditional 'A' levels is well known, who vetoed the Higginson proposals. It was reported that Kenneth Baker had earlier given verbal assurances to Professor Higginson that the recommendations for a five subject system were acceptable. There was widespread disappointment amongst a wide spectrum of professional educationists that this opportunity for reform had been missed. The need for greater breadth at this level of study had been very widely acknowledged by those involved in industry and commerce as well as education. Now it seems likely that an examination structure designed for the 1950s, with its limited range of subjects which is out of line with practice in the rest of the world, will survive until at least the end of the century. It is doubtful whether its continued existence in its present form will be able to meet adequately the needs of a modern economy for young people with considerable intellectual flexibility.

Vocational qualifications, in contrast, have experienced major review in the mid-1980s and are undergoing considerable reorganisation at present. Full- and part-time vocational and professional courses still constitute the 'bread and butter' work of the further education colleges. There are five major national examining and validating bodies operating in the vocational field and also six regional examining boards. In addition, there are about 250 professional bodies and about 120 industry training organisations all engaged in accrediting and examining their own qualifications. It has been difficult for specialists and impossible for ordinary citizens to see their way through these complex structures. In 1986, under the auspices of the DES and the MSC, a Review of Vocational Qualifications was conducted under the chairmanship of Oscar De Ville.[28] Its main recommendation was the setting up of the National Council for Vocational Qualifications (NCVQ) which has been implemented. This new body does not award qualifications itself but performs a quality control function. It has the power to regulate vocational examining and, in future, awarding bodies will need its stamp of approval. NCVQ has also been given the task of organising and ordering the hundreds of qualifications that are offered in this area. It is required to divide these qualifications into a new framework of four hierarchical categories. The four levels will denote different standards, and descriptions of them are given below. The De Ville Report was unable to give precise guidance beyond level IV, but felt that level V 'should reflect competence at professional level'.[29]

Level	Description of Standard[30]
I	Occupational competence in performing a range of tasks under supervision.
II	Occupational competence in performing a wider range of more demanding tasks with limited supervision.
III	Occupational competence required for satisfactory, responsible performance in a defined occupation or range of jobs.
IV	Competence to design and specify tasks, products or processes and to accept responsibility for the work of others.

NCVQ is still working on this categorisation, but it is hoped and expected that when the task is complete, the result will help the one and a half million consumers of vocational education to understand the system and enable them to see how their own courses fit into the national framework. 'A' levels do not come within the terms of reference of the NCVQ, and it is likely that the existing divide between the 'academic' and the 'vocational' routes into higher education and professional qualifications will continue in the foreseeable future.

In recent years one institution which has attempted to bridge the false divide between the 'academic' and the 'vocational' has been the tertiary college. There are now over forty such colleges in England and Wales. They operate under FE regulations and they provide a full range of full- and part-time courses for students over 16 years of age who are not in institutions of higher education. Often they provide a wide variety of activities in adult education, including non-vocational courses. It has been said quite accurately that they are not just for the 16–19s but for the 16–90s. Normally a tertiary college is the sole provider of post-16 education in its catchment area.

Tertiary colleges offer a number of advantages as a form of organisation for post-16 education. Their size enables them to offer a wide range of courses and subjects; for example, they are often able to run more 'A' level options than a school sixth form.

Size also normally offers economies of scale, and numbers in teaching groups can be kept at a viable level. Tertiary colleges are comprehensive post-16 institutions that are unselective in their intakes. YTS trainees can be studying in the same institution as Oxbridge entry candidates. Butchers and bankers attend alongside the unemployed. If at the age of 16 students proceed from secondary school to tertiary college, they can concentrate on finding the most appropriate courses for themselves without worrying about the relative statuses of the institutions available. Careers teachers in schools can give impartial advice more easily as they no longer have to be concerned about recruiting sixth formers for their own institutions. The potentially wasteful competition that can exist between schools and FE is ended. Tertiary colleges were often in a good position to offer unconventional combinations of studies, and students can more easily arrange transfers between courses if the complications of moving from one institution to another are avoided. Post-16 colleges are able to provide an adult atmosphere for their studies. They do not need to be concerned with discipline in the way that schools dealing with younger pupils have to be, and they can allow their students much more scope to arrange their own lives and affairs. Those who work in tertiary colleges claim that their examination results ('A' levels are often taken as the yardstick) are as good as, if not better than, those achieved in schools.

Those who oppose tertiary reorganisation tend to stress a number of factors. They claim that the size of the colleges is likely to make them impersonal. It is suggested that schools have been more successful in developing pastoral care and counselling systems than further education, although this is hotly disputed by those who work in the latter sector. College liaison with feeder schools can never be as smooth as students progressing from the fifth to the sixth form in the same institution. The break at 16 is an unnecessary intrusion into the continuity of the educational process, and, as most students remain in the college for two years or less, there is too little time for students to build up much affinity with their new institutions. Parents sometimes express concern that opportunities for leadership available in the traditional sixth form are lost in the college setting, and some parents fear that the atmosphere in colleges is too relaxed, preventing students from concentrating on serious study. There can be little doubt that there are also parents who do not want their offspring, even when they are over 16, to mix with the full range of people in the community which a tertiary college accommodates. They would prefer a more restricted and protected environment. The effects of tertiary reorganisation on schools which lose their sixth forms also have to be considered. There are, without doubt, good teachers who make excellent contributions to the education of both sixth formers and younger pupils. They will have their opportunities to continue to do both curtailed. It is possible that 11–16 schools will find it more difficult to recruit staff in shortage subjects than 11–18 schools, although there is not much evidence to substantiate this at present.

The politics of tertiary reorganisation is an interesting topic in its own right. The Labour Party and the Liberals have shown considerable interest in tertiary schemes for some time. The Conservatives have been more sceptical although tertiary colleges have emerged in a number of staunchly Conservative LEAs. In the early days of the Thatcher Government a national committee chaired by the then Minister of State, Neil MacFarlane, considered 16–19 education.[31] Evidence suggests that this committee was about to report favourably concerning tertiary colleges and their future development, but senior Conservatives, possibly including Margaret Thatcher herself, intervened. When the report eventually appeared, it was couched in bland terms which would not cause offence to the school sixth-form lobby. Later, in 1986, it looked as if the DES was beginning to look favourably again on tertiary schemes, but in Circular 3/87 the Government avoided firm commitment to any particular form of 16–19 organisation. It has indicated that it has 'no preferred solution' and that it will consider various arrangements as long as they are 'well adapted to local circumstances'.[32] The Education Reform Act of 1988, with the possibility of the emergence of 'opted out' Grant Maintained schools, has probably put more obstacles in the way of tertiary reorganisation schemes. During 1988 Kenneth Baker and Angela Rumbold made it clear that they saw FE colleges as providers of vocational courses for industry rather than as an alternative road to higher education. They seemed intent on perpetuating, even reinforcing, the existing divide between 'academic' and 'vocational' provisions. As has been pointed out,[33] this policy does not rest easily with the Government's own TVEI scheme. The mix of 'academic', 'technological' and 'vocational' courses in the tertiary college concept may soon be overshadowed by the prospect of 11–18 Grant Maintained schools and City Technology colleges. Some years ago Stuart Ranson wrote of the possibility of 'tertiary tripartism' in 16–19 education.[34] This looks even more likely now. The 'grammar' streams will be found in the sixth forms of Independent and Grant Maintained schools and sixth-form colleges. The 'technical' streams will be located in the City Technology colleges and the craft classes in FE colleges. The 'modern' streams will consist of CPVE students and YTS trainees who will train 'on the job' and in the FE colleges. This part of the education service could easily become as stratified as it was during the 1950s.

It is now widely recognised that Britain has one of the lowest participation rates in 16–19 education in the developed world. It is difficult to quote statistics which make meaningful comparisons between countries, but study after study has shown how Britain lags behind its major industrial competitors such as West Germany, France, the USA and Japan. All the major political parties indicate that they are committed to improve these rates as it is believed that low participation in education and training during these crucial years have contributed to this country's poor economic performance in the post-war years. During the 1980s demography has ensured that there has been a plentiful supply of 16–19 year olds available, and in many respects the depressed British economy has found it difficult to accommodate all those available for work. The number of 16–19 year olds is now falling rapidly and will continue to do so in the early 1990s. According to Anne Jones, director of educational programmes at the Training Agency, one consequence of this will be that by 1992 '16–18s will be like gold dust. Employers will fall over themselves to employ them and youth unemployment will disappear.'[35] In these circumstances it could be difficult to persuade young people to stay in education and training when highly paid dead-end jobs are available. These demographic factors will operate across the whole spectrum, and it may prove a particular problem to recruit young people to the relatively long training courses which lead to the modestly paid caring professions. Given the unfavourable context of the early 1990s, it may be a struggle to sustain even our current low rates of participation in 16–19 education and training.

At the local level further education has been administered by the LEAs for a very long time. To try to provide better regional coordination between neighbouring LEAs in further education the Regional Advisory Councils (RACs) were set up in 1947–48. There are nine RACs in England and one in Wales. The RACs are financed and, in practice, controlled by their constitutent LEAs although other bodies are represented on them. They seek to avoid the unnecessary duplication of courses and facilities in their regions and also attempt to promote greater cooperation in a positive sense. In the 1986 Education Act the Government encouraged greater 'free trade' between LEAs in Non-Advanced Further Education (NAFE). Prior to this legislation a student who lived in the area of one LEA and attended a NAFE course in another had to obtain the consent of his or her home authority before recoupment (inter-authority payment) was made. Now students interested in most NAFE courses have free choice between institutions irrespective of the LEAs in which they are situated. Their home authority is obliged automatically to reimburse the LEA providing the course place. Thus, FE colleges now have added incentive to market their courses as attractively and as widely as practicable.

The relationship between an FE college and its LEA is mediated through its governing body. In general, college governing bodies have been allowed rather more scope than those of schools, but practices have varied considerably between different LEAs. Since 1970 colleges have normally had academic boards containing representatives of teaching staff. The function of these boards has been to advise principals on the development of the academic and professional work of the colleges. The membership of college governing bodies has varied in different parts of the country according to local traditions, but it has been common for LEA representatives to be in the majority. The 1988 Education Reform Act has amended these arrangements and considerably weakened the LEA position. In future not more than 20 per cent of the members of college governing bodies will be appointed by LEAs and at least 50 per cent will be representatives of employment interests or co-opted members. The DES is required to approve the composition of governing bodies which will have a maximum of 25 members. It has been suggested by the Department that a typical governing body might be composed as follows:[36]

12	representatives of business, industrial, professional and employment interests, including not more than 2 from trade unions
4	representatives of the LEA
2	representatives of parents
2	members drawn from neighbouring educational institutions
2	representatives of the staff (teaching and non-teaching)
1	representative of the students
1	principal
24	Total

In this way the Government intends to ensure that industrial and business people have a major influence in the running of the colleges and that LEA power is simultaneously reduced. In essence, the predominance of one interest group is to be replaced by that of another.

For some years many colleges, through their governing bodies, have exercised some control over their budgets. The Government wants them to build on this experience, and believes that they 'should be given as much freedom as possible to manage their own affairs and decide their own priorities for spending the resources allocated to them'.[37] The 1988 Act introduces financial delegation for colleges in much the same way as it does for schools. An account of the provisions for financial delegation is included in Chapter 5. The requirement in the 1944 Act that LEAs should produce schemes for further education is repealed in the new legislation, as are the sections relating to the establishment of county colleges which have never been put into operation. In line with the general thrust of the 1988 Education Reform Act, the role of LEAs in planning and controlling NAFE is significantly reduced and the position of college governing bodies, now potentially dominated by business interests, enhanced. It is to be hoped that the interests of students and staff are not forgotten in the struggles for power and influence which may ensue in the 1990s.

It is now time to turn from NAFE to its counterpart AFE (Advanced Further Education). NAFE is normally defined as education up to and including 'A' level or its equivalent, and AFE as qualifications above 'A' level standard or its equivalent. AFE and NAFE are both quite commonly taught in the same institutions, but in the last twenty years a number of distinct AFE polytechnics and colleges have been developed. These are often referred to collectively as 'the public sector of higher education', and they are on the opposite side of the so-called 'binary line' in higher education to the universities.

Recently the Government has pointed out that it .finds the description 'public sector of higher education' unhelpful.[38] It stresses that the universities are also heavily dependent on public funds and that it wants both the universities and other institutions of higher education to attract more private funding. It suggests that in future the term 'polytechnics and colleges sector' should replace 'public sector'. Since the mid-1960s degrees and other awards in this sector of education have been validated by the Council for National Academic Awards (CNAA) although some universities are also involved in this work to some extent.

In 1987 in England and Wales 427 institutions outside of the universities provided higher education courses. These included 30 polytechnics, 366 other colleges under LEAs (some of which provided a comparatively small number of higher education courses) and 31 colleges financed directly by the DES or the Welsh Office (these included 18 voluntary colleges originally set up by the Churches to train teachers). Since the late 1960s this sector has been led, in effect, by the polytechnics and has been dominated by institutions under LEA control. There was and is much less emphasis on research in these institutions than in the universities and they have been developed primarily as teaching institutions. Although other points of contrast with the universities have often been mentioned, these have not been fully substantiated nor consistently pursued. In the 1970s the old LEA traditions in advanced work – technical colleges and teacher training – were merged in several of the growing polytechnics and in the new colleges (or institutes) of higher education. As students were recruited to these institutions from all parts of the country, it was important to share the costs fairly between all LEAs to ensure that the burden did not fall disproportionately on the providing authorities. Consequently 'pools' were set up (separate ones for England and Wales), and LEAs contributed to their appropriate pool according to a formula. The money was then allocated to the providing authorities to cover their higher education course costs. From 1980 these pools were 'capped' (the total amount in them was controlled by central government) so that LEAs were not required to meet an annual open-ended commitment of resources over which most of them had little influence. Despite this and other expenditure controls imposed in the 1980s, polytechnics and colleges have continued to recruit and educate more students thus progressively reducing their 'unit of resource'. The major bone of contention in this sector ever since its creation has been the question of who should control it. The LEAs have maintained that as the main providing bodies they should be permitted to develop their own institutions in their own way, but senior DES civil servants, with varying support from ministers, have stressed that there was need for much more effective national leadership, planning and management in this expensive sector of education. Various solutions and compromises were canvassed throughout the 1970s but no lasting agreement could be found. During 1980–81 DES civil servants came up with proposals to rationalise and contract this sector and at the same time to remove a large number of polytechnics and colleges from local authority control. These ideas were strongly resisted by the LEAs, and different Conservative Party educationists had very different views on them. Eventually a compromise was reached in 1981 with the setting up of the National Advisory Body for Local Authority Higher Education (later extended to the voluntary colleges, and in 1985 renamed the National Advisory Body for Public Sector Higher Education which was to advise the Government on planning and funding. In many ways this structure preserved the local authority stake in higher education largely giving LEAs what they wanted. Given the Thatcher Government's general attitude to local government, it was surprising that the LEAs obtained such a victory in 1981, but it has proved short lived as the White Paper of 1987, *Higher Education: Meeting the Challenge*[39] and the Education Reform Act of 1988 show most comprehensively and conclusively.

The 1988 Act has taken nearly fifty polytechnics and colleges out of LEA control and has incorporated them with charitable status to provide higher (including further) education and to carry out research. Seven smaller colleges with fewer than 350 AFE students will be similarly incorporated with the agreement of their LEAs. To qualify for incorporation colleges had to have more than 55 per cent of their full-time equivalent student numbers on AFE courses. The new higher education corporations control the lands and properties of their institutions and they employ the staff. They form the boards of governors which consist of between thirteen and twenty-five members including the principal unless he or she chooses not to serve. The initial members are appointed by the Secretary of State and they include people with experience of industry, business commerce and the professions (half the total approximately), teaching and non-teaching staff, student and local authority nominees and members co-opted by the rest of the board. Initially these arrangements apply to England only, but the Secretary of State for Wales has been given the power to introduce them there later without the need for further legislation. It is intended that the governors will 'have wide powers to determine the affairs of the institution. The Director of each institution will report only to the Governors.'[40] Further changes have been made to the national administrative machinery. The National Advisory Board has been disbanded and the pooling arrangements abolished. The Polytechnics and Colleges Funding Council (PCFC) has been established to replace these former structures. The PCFC controls the funding of the newly incorporated institutions and the former Direct Grant colleges. Its members are appointed by the Secretary of State and the Council comprises between six and nine persons experienced in higher education as well as members who are familiar with industry, commerce and finance. The Council receives funds from central government for the purposes of education and research, and it is empowered to make grants to individual institutions according to any terms and conditions it thinks fit. Central planning and management have at last been achieved in this sector of higher education which should please those at the DES who have sought it for nearly twenty years.

On the other side of the 'binary line' there are thirty-five universities in England and Wales (excluding the Open University and the University of Buckingham which does not receive public funds). The universities operate under their own charters and have considerable academic freedom. Some of the largest universities have over ten thousand students. This sector concentrates largely on honours degree courses, postgraduate work and research. For many years the bulk of the funds for the universities came from central government through the University Grants Committee (UGC) which was set up as early as 1919. The UGC was intended to form a buffer between autonomous higher education institutions on the one hand and central government funding on the other. For much of this century it was felt necessary to protect the academic freedom of the universities from the potential interference of a central government holding the purse strings. In more recent times there has been some feeling in Government circles that universities are rather extravagant institutions which need to direct their attention to stricter financial management and which have used the academic freedom argument to avoid justifiable accountability. The Secretary of State appointed UGC members, who served in individual rather than representative capacities, from both higher education and business. The UGC was responsible, in effect, for examining the financial needs of individual universities and for allocating grants to them. It could initiate developments and organise rationalisation programmes throughout the sector. In 1981, for example, it implemented major restructuring or, according to one's perspective, imposed draconian cuts. In the mid-1980s it instituted the 'new blood' and information technology programmes which aimed to bring able young recruits in natural science and technology into university service. During the mid-1980s much emphasis has been laid on efficiency and effective management of resources along the lines of the recommendations of the Jarratt Committee.[41] In many ways this led to the setting up of a committee chaired by Lord Croham to review the UGC's constitutional position and role. The Croham Report[42] was published in February 1987 and proposed the creation of a new independent body to control university finances. The Government has accepted many, but not all, of Croham's ideas, and several of them have been included in the 1988 Education Reform Act. The UGC is to be abolished and replaced by a new Universities Funding Council (UFC). The UFC is to be constituted on the same lines as the PCFC, already discussed, and it will perform similar functions for the university sector. Some commentators believe that in the longer term a merger between the PCFC and the UFC, with their similar terms of reference, is a likely development, and thus a unitary system of higher education will emerge.

The Government has made it clear that it intends to introduce a new approach to funding higher education as soon as possible. It points out that the emphasis on grants from public funds in the past does not imply 'unconditional entitlement to support from the taxpayer at any particular level'.[43] The Government wants to replace grants with a system of contracting between the institutions and the new funding bodies. Universities, polytechnics and colleges will be encouraged to try to attract contracts from the private sector and thus lessen their dependence on public funding.[44] Details of how a system of contracting will be operated in practice still have to be clarified, but the Government has indicated that it is not using the term 'contracts' in a strict legal sense. At the same time Training Agency funding is beginning to affect higher education in the late 1980s[45] and this could result in radically new developments. Some university vice-chancellors are developing ideas for student vouchers to fund higher education. In such a scheme State grants would largely be replaced by vouchers awarded to potential students to spend on degree courses in the institutions of their choice. This would place higher education institutions in a much more competitive position, and the Government has shown some interest in these notions. At the same time the Government considered how student maintenance grants, which for some years had failed to keep pace with inflation, could best be replaced by loans. In 1988 a scheme was published which proposed to freeze grants at their current level and introduce top-up loans. Repayments will depend on an individual's economic circumstances. When the scheme is introduced, students will lose their rights to claim benefits. The Government believe that this is 'an important step away from the dependency culture', but is strongly opposed by the students.

It is appropriate to conclude this chapter with a brief mention of recent developments in the initial training of teachers. There are currently two major routes into teaching – three- or four-year BEd courses and one-year postgraduate certificates in education. Universities, polytechnics and colleges are all involved in the provision of these qualifications. Initial training courses require the approval of the Secretary of State, and, following DES Circular 3/84[46], the Council for the Accreditation of Teacher Education (CATE) was established to scrutinise provisions to ensure that they met the relatively stringent criteria set out in the circular. The need to meet the requirements of CATE has already led to course revisions involving greater emphasis on practice in school and to the implementation of programmes which enable teacher trainers to return to the classroom to update their experience. CATE is to be wound up, but it is likely that it will be superseded by a new body with powers to apply even stronger criteria in this area of course approval. In a recent consultation paper, *Qualified Teacher Status*,[47] the DES has set out proposals which, if implemented, could revolutionise entry into the teaching profession in England and Wales. The document states that it seeks merely to simplify the complicated procedures for entry into teaching for those who lack the standard qualifications. It proposes that, in future, employers (LEAs or governing bodies in the case of Aided or Grant Maintained schools) be empowered to grant licences to teach to individuals with suitable educational qualifications above 'A' level. They would also be responsible for making some training arrangements for licensed teachers in their employment. After two years' teaching experience and an appropriate recommendation from the employer, a licensed teacher would be awarded qualified teacher status. It is also suggested that the current statutory arrangements for the probation of teachers should be withdrawn and the responsibility for monitoring the performance of new teachers should pass entirely to the employers. Although it is claimed that these arrangements are intended for the benefit of only a small number of potential teachers, there seems no reason, if the Government so wishes, to prevent them from being developed into a standard route into teaching. They could easily serve this purpose as they stand, and they could cut training costs substantially as the courses offered by the current training institutions could be short-circuited. There could also be considerable appeal in such arrangements to those contemplating teaching, perhaps particularly to mature people already in other jobs. Direct entry into paid employment in teaching would be possible, and new entrants would not have to worry about living on grants or negotiating loans for the duration of their training courses. It is possible that the Government sees these measures as part of its strategy to overcome the difficulty of recruiting sufficient teachers to implement the National Curriculum in the early 1990s. There is wide agreement that there are likely to be major problems in obtaining the teachers: particularly in the well-known shortage subjects. If this is the Government's intention, the price of the National Curriculum will be the dilution of standards in the teaching profession. This could easily produce equally sad consequences for both pre- and post-16 education in this country.

REFERENCES

1. DES, 1987 Circular 3/87, *Providing for Quality: The Pattern of Organisation to Age 19*, HMSO p. 5.
2. *Ibid.*, p. 2.
3. *Ibid.*, p. 6.
4. DES, 1985 *Better Schools*, HMSO.
5. DES, 1986 Draft Circular, HMSO.
6. DES, Circular 3/87, *op. cit.* p. 5.
7. *Ibid.*
8. DES, 1982 Circular 4/82, *Statutory Proposals for Secondary Schools and Falling Rolls*.
9. *Ibid.*
10. DES, Circular 3/87, *op. cit.* p. 1.
11. *Ibid.*, p. 6.
12. DES, 1988 *Sixth Form Colleges in England*, Report of HMI, HMSO, p. 2.
13. DES, *Projected Numbers of Students in Maintained Colleges Studying on Non-Advanced Courses: England: 1986–2000*, HMSO, p. 5.

14. *Ibid.*, p. 1.
15. T. Sharpe, 1976 *Wilt*, Pan Books.
16. DES, 1987 Statistical Bulletin 2/87.
17. Department of Employment, 1981 *A New Training Initiative*, HMSO.
18. Department of Employment/DES, 1984 *Training for Jobs*, HMSO.
19. *Ibid.*
20. A. Thomson and H. Rosenberg, 1986 *A User's Guide to the Manpower Services Commission*, p. 24.
21. Manpower Service Commission, *Annual Report 1986/7*, p. 26.
22. Deloitte, Haskins and Sell, (Management Consultancy Division), 1987 *The Funding of Vocational Education and Training: Report to the* Manpower Services Commission.
23. HMI, 1987 *NAFE in Practice*, HMSO.
24. Department of Employment, 1988 *Employment in the 1990s*, HMSO.
25. Further Education Unit, 1979 *A Basis for Choice*.
26. DES, 1988 *Advancing A Levels*, p. 39. Terms of reference of the Higginson Committee.
27. DES, 1988 *Advancing A Levels*, HMSO, Report of Committee – Chairman, G. R. H. Higginson.
28. DES/MSC, 1986 *Review of Vocational Qualifications*, A Report of Working Group – Chairman O. De Ville, HMSO.
29. *Ibid.*
30. *Ibid.*
31. DES/ Local Authority Associations, 1980 *Education for 16–19 year olds*, A Review for the Government and the Local Authority Associations – Chairman N. MacFarlane, HMSO.
32. DES, Circular 3/87, *op.cit.*, p. 5.
33. Education, 18 March 1988.
34. S. Ranson, 1984 'Towards a Tertiary Tripartism', in P. Broadfoot (ed.), *Selection, Certification and Control*, Falmer Press.
35. Education, 20 May 1988.
36. DES, 1987 *Maintained Further Education: Financing, Governance and Law*, HMSO, August, p. 14.
37. *Ibid.*, p. 5.
38. DES, 1987 *Higher Education: Meeting the Challenge*, HMSO, April, p. 25.
39. DES, 1987 *Higher Education: Meeting the Challenge*, HMSO.
40 *Ibid.*, p. 30.
41. Committee of Vice-Chancellors and Principals, 1985 *Efficiency Studies in Universities, Report of Steering Committee – Chairman Sir A. Jarratt.*
42. University Grants Committee, 1987 *Review of the University Grants Committee*, Report of Group – Chairman Lord Croham.
43. *Ibid.*, p. 31.
44. *Ibid.*
45. MSC, 1988 *University, Enterprise and Local Economic Development*, Report by Segal Quince Wickstead.
46. DES, 1984 Circular 3/84, *Initial Teacher Training: Approval of Courses*, HMSO.
47. DES, 1988 *Qualified Teacher Status: Consultation Document*, HMSO.

FURTHER READING

Benn, C. and Fairley, J. 1986 *Challenging the MSC*, Photo Press.
Cantor, L. M. and Roberts, I. F. 1986 *Further Education Today*, Routledge and Kegan Paul.
DES, Circular 3/87 1987 *Providing for Quality: The Pattern of Organisation to Age 19*, HMSO.
DES 1988 *Advancing A Levels*, HMSO.
DES 1987 *Higher Education: Meeting the Challenge*, HMSO.
Department of Employment/DES 1984 *Training for Jobs*, HMSO.
Department of Employment 1988 *Employment in the 1990s*, HMSO.
Further Education Unit 1979 *A Basis for Choice*, FEU.
Her Majesty's Inspectors 1987 *NAFE in Practice*, HMSO.
Lambert S. 1988 *Managing Tertiary and Sixth Form Colleges*, Longman.
MSC/DES 1986 *Review of Vocational Qualifications*, HMSO.
Ranson S. 1984 'Towards a Tertiary Tripartism', in P. Broadfood, *Selection, Certification and Control*, Falmer Press.
Ranson, S., Taylor, B. and Brighouse, T. (1986) *The Revolution in Education and Training*, Longman.
Sharp, P. R. 1987 *The Creation of the Local Authority Sector of Higher Education*, Falmer Press.
Terry, D. 1987 *The Tertiary College*, Open University Press.

BIBLIOGRAPHY

Association of County Councils, 1987 *Understanding Block Grants 1987–88*.
Audit Commission, 1984 *Obtaining Better Value in Education: Aspects of Non-Teaching Costs in Secondary Schools*.
Audit Commission, 1985 *Obtaining Value for Further Education*.
Audit Commission, 1986 *Towards Better Management of Secondary Education*.
Baron G and Howell D A, 1974 *The Government and Management of Schools* Athlone Press.
Benn C and Fairley J, 1986 *Challenging the MSC* Photo Press.
Board of Education, 1926 *The Education of the Adolescent* (Report of Consultative Commitee on Education, Chairman Sir W. H. Hadow).
Board of Education, 1938 *Secondary Education with special reference to Grammar Schools and Technical High Schools* (Report of Consultative Committee on Education, Chairman W. Spens).
Boyle, Lord E, 1972 'The Politics of Secondary School Reorganisation: some Reflections'. *Journal of Educational Administration and History*
Brighouse T, 1986 'What can be done about central control' *Education* **165**
Brooksbank K and Ackstine A, 1989 *Educational Administration* Councils and Educational Press.
Bush T and Kogan M, 1982 *Directors of Education*, Allen and Unwin.
Cantor L M and Roberts I F, 1986 *Further Education Today* Routledge and Kegan Paul.
Committee of Vice-Chancellors and Principals, 1985 *Efficiency Studies in Universities* (Report of Steering Committee – Chairman Sir A Jarratt).
Central Advisory Council for Education, 1967 *Children and their Primary Schools* (Report of Committee Chair Lady B. Plowden).
Cooke G and Gosden P, 1986 *Education Committees*, Councils and Educational Press.
Coopers and Lybrand Associates, 1987 *Local Management of Schools: Report to the DES* Coopers and Lybrand.
Deloitte, Haskins and Sells, 1987 *The Funding of Vocational Education and Training: Report to the MSC* Manpower Services Commission.
Dennison W F, 1984 *Educational Finance and Resources* Croom Helm.
DES, 1965 Circular 10/65 *The Organisation of Secondary Education*, HMSO.
DES, 1970 Circular 10/70 *The Organisation of Secondary Education*, HMSO.

DES, 1978 *The Composition of Governing Bodies, HMSO.*

DES, 1982 Circular 4/82 Statutory Proposals for Secondary Schools and Falling Rolls, HMSO.

DES, 1983 *Study of HMI in England and Wales*, HMSO.

DES, 1984 Circular 3/84 *Initial Teacher Training: Approval of Courses*, HMSO.

DES, 1985 *The DES – A Brief Guide*, HMSO.

DES, 1985 *Better Schools*, HMSO.

DES, 1986 Draft Circular, August, HMSO.

DES, Statistical Bulletin 2/87 March, HMSO.

DES, Statistical Bulletin 14/87 December, HMSO.

DES, 1987 Circular 3/87 *Providing for Quality: The Pattern of Organisation to Age 19.* HMSO.

DES, 1987 *Higher Education; Meeting the Challenge* HMSO.

DES, 1987 *Teachers' Pay and Conditions. A Consultative Document* HMSO.

DES, 1987 *Maintained Further Education: Financing, Governance and Law*, HMSO.

DES, 1988 Circular 7/88 *Local Management of Schools*, HMSO.

DES, 1988 *Advancing A Levels* HMSO.

DES, 1988 *Sixth Form Colleges in England* Report of HMI, HMSO.

DES, 1988 *Qualified Teacher Status; Consultation Document*, HMSO.

DES, (latest edn available) *School Teachers' Pay and Conditions Document*, HMSO.

DES/Local Authority Associations, 1980 *Education for 16–19 year olds.* (A Review for the Government and the Local Authority Associations – Chairman N. MacFarlane), HMSO.

DES/MSC, 1986 *Review of Vocational Qualifications* (A Report of Working Group – Chairman O. De Ville), HMSO.

DES, *Projected Numbers of Students in Maintained Colleges Studying on Non-Advanced Courses: England 1986–2000*, HMSO.

Department of Employment, 1981 *A New Training Initiative* HMSO.

Department of Employment/DES, 1984 *Training for Jobs* HMSO.

Department of Employment, 1988 *Employment in the 1990s* HMSO.

Department of Environment, 1986 *Paying for Local Government* HMSO

Education, March 1988.

Education, May 1988

Education Act, 1980 Schedule 2 Part II s. 6.

Education Act, 1981

Evans K, 1985 *The Development and Structure of the English School System* Hodder and Stoughton.

Fenwick I and McBride P, 1982 *The Government of Education in Britain* Martin Robertson.

Fiske D, 1979 *Journal of National Association of Inspectors and Educational Advisers.*

Further Education Unit, 1979 *A Basis for Choice*, FEU.

Gosden P H J H, 1966 *The Development of Educational Administration in England and Wales* Blackwell.

Gosden P H J H, 1976 *Education in the Second World War*, Methuen.

Gosden P H J H, 1983 *The Education System since 1944* Martin Roberston.

Gosden P H J H 1985 'Education Policy 1979–84 in D Bell (ed.) *The Conservative Government 1979–84 An Interim Report* Croom Helm
Her Majesty's Inspectors, 1987 *NAFE in Practice* HMSO.
House of Commons Bill, 1981 *Education: A Bill to make provision with respect to children with special educational needs*, HMSO.
Lambert S, 1988 *Managing Tertiary and Sixth Form Colleges* Longman.
Lawson J and Silver H, 1973 *A Social History of Education in England* Methuen.
Lawton D and Gordon P, 1987 *HMI* Routledge and Kegan-Paul.
Lowe R, 1988 *Education in the Post-war Years* Routledge.
MacClure S, 1988 *Education Reformed* Hodder and Stoughton.
Manpower Services Commission, *Annual Reports*
Manpower Services Commission, 1988 *University, Enterprise and Local Economic Development* (Report by Segal Quince Wickstead).
Pile W, 1979 *The Department of Education and Science* Allen and Unwin.
Ranson S, 1984 'Towards a Tertiary Tripartism' in P. Broadfoot (ed) *Selection Certification and Control* Falmer Press.
Ranson S Taylor B and Brighouse T, 1986 *The Revolution in Education and Training* Longman.
Ranson S and Tomlinson J, (eds) 1986 *The Changing Government of Education* Allen and Unwin.
Regan D, 1984 *Local Government and Education* Allen and Unwin.
Salter B and Tapper, T 1981 *Education, Politics and the State* Grant McIntyre.
Sanderson M, 1987 *Educational Opportunity* Faber and Faber.
Sharp P R, 1987 *The Creation of the Local Authority Sector of Higher Education* Falmer Press.
Sharpe T, 1976 *Wilt* Pan Books.
Stillman A and Maychell K, 1986 *Choosing Schools: Parents LEAs and the 1980 Education Act* NFER/Nelson.
Terry D, 1987 *The Tertiary College* Open University Press.
Thompson A and Rosenberg H, 1986 *A User's Guide to the Manpower Services Commission*.
Treasury, 1987 Economic Progress Report 189, *The Budget*, HMSO.
University Grants Committee, 1987 *Review of the University Grants Committee* (Report of Group – Chairman Lord Croham).
West E G, 1965 *Education and the State* Institute of Economic Affairs.
West E G, 1975 *Education and the Industrial Revolution* Batsford.
Winckley C, 1985 *Diplomats and Detectives* Roberts Royce.

INDEX

'A' levels, 94–7, 103, 105, 106–7,
    108, 109, 113
academic qualifications-sale of, 45
Acts of Parliament
    (non-educational)
    *Educational Acts are
    indexed under 'E'*
    Reform Act 1867, 8
    Board of Education Act 1899, 12
    Local Government Act 1963, 61
    Industrial Training Act 1964, 98
    Local Government Act 1972,
        26, 61, 62
    Employment and Training Act
        1973, 98
    Local Government Finance Act
        1982, 38
    Rates Act 1984, 85
    Local Government Finance Act
        1988, 86, 87, 92
adult education, 108
Advanced/Supplementary (AS)
    levels, 105–6, 107
Advisers/Inspectors (LEA), 70–1
Alexander, Lord William, 57, 58,
    74
Anglesey LEA, 22
appeals
    under 1944 Education Act, 29
    under 1980 Education Act,
        29–30
    under 1981 Education Act, 33–4
    under 1986 Education Act, 37
apprentiscehips, 98, 99, 100
Arnold, Thomas, 94
Assistant Masters and Mistresses
    Association, 77
assisted places scheme, 29, 32, 49,
    91
Association of County Councils, 84

Association of Education
    Committees, 26, 48, 57, 74,
    82
attendance
    compulsory, 9
Audit Commission, 38–9, 89

Baines Report, 62, 67
Baker, Kenneth, 40, 90, 107, 110
Blackburn County Borough LEA,
    27
Board of Education, 12, 13, 15,
    16, 17, 18, 20, 47
Board of Trade, 9
Boyle, Edward, 22, 23
Bradford LEA, 37
British and Foreign School
    Society, 3
Burnham Committee, 76–7, 78, 79
Business Education Council, 98
Business/Technician Education
    Council (BTEC), 59, 94,
    98, 104
Butler, R. A. (Rab), 17

Callaghan, James, 26, 52, 56, 58
Cambridgeshire LEA, 90
central schools, 15
Certificate of Extended Education
    (CEE), 103, 104
Certificate of Pre-Vocational
    Education, 104–5, 110
Certificate of Secondary
    Education (CSE), 58, 104
chambers of commerce, 103
Charity Commission, 10, 11, 12
chief education officers, 42, 56, 67
Church of England, 3, 5
City and Guilds of London
    Institute, 59, 94, 98, 103–4